An Experience Of Celibacy

A creative reflection on intimacy, loneliness, sexuality and commitment

Keith Clark, Capuchin

Ave Maria Press   Notre Dame, Indiana

Imprimi Potest: Ronald Smith, Capuchin
Minister Provincial
The Province of St. Joseph
Detroit, Michigan
June 26, 1981

Acknowledgments: Scripture texts used in this work are taken from the NEW AMERICAN BIBLE, copyright © 1970, by the Confraternity of Christian Doctrine, Washington, D.C., and are used by permission of copyright owner. All rights reserved.

International Standard Book Number: 0-87793-239-5 (Cloth)
0-87793-240-9 (Paper)

Library of Congress Catalog Card Number: 81-69747

Printed and bound in the United States of America.

Text and Cover Design: Elizabeth French

I respectfully dedicate this work
to those from whom I learned celibacy—
    my mother and father,
    and those many students
        who thought *they* were learning from *me*;

and to the Parkers—four generations of them—
    who helped me appreciate realistically
    the beauty of the life I have not chosen.

♣ Contents

♣ Foreword

Today is my 40th birthday. Earlier I was thinking, "I've planted my tree and I've written my book." Of the three things I've been told that every man wants to do in his life, I've done two. The third, to have a child, I've decided not to do.

I learned a lot from planting a tree. I learned that it takes a long time for some seeds to germinate, and that it takes patience and hope. I learned that from the chestnuts I planted 10 years ago.

Planting a tree also indicates belief in life—life beyond our own allotted days. The tiny sapling, watched over in curiosity and amazement, will itself stand over and give shade to generations not yet born.

I learned that a tree—a sapling whose roots have outgrown the confinement of the pot in which it was originally planted—wilts when transplanted. And that helped me with my own transplantings as I was uprooted from familiar surroundings and asked to sink my roots in new soil and develop new relationships.

From planting a tree I learned that for all the patience, care, hope and even worry that go into the beginning of a tree's life, its final fate, once you've committed it to the soil outside, is dependent on a lot of forces other than your own. The tree I planted next to a bathhouse in Indiana was mowed over two years in a row by an ambitious but careless brother. It came up again the following year, but eventually died. But if I hadn't transplanted it outside, it would have died from the confinement of its original pot. At least it died outside where it belonged, not in the stifling security of the pot in my room. And from that I think I learned something.

I also learned something from writing a book, *Make Space, Make Symbols*, several years ago. I learned it takes work and discipline, not just an idea and a dream. I learned that its conception and birth require the cooperation of a lot of people besides the author. I learned that the author requires more gentle treatment than the book does. And I was treated gently.

I learned from writing a book that ideas and their expression, which at one time seemed large enough to fill one's entire thoughts, diminish in importance with the passage of time. The ideas which preoccupied me while I was trying to find an adequate expression of them had been joined by new thoughts and ideas before the book was published. They didn't seem so large then; still good, but terribly relative in their importance to me. I was left on publishing date with the same doubts I had had when I began writing: Is it worth bothering people with the ideas? But the machinery was grinding out the books and the system was preparing to bring them into people's hands and the ideas before their minds.

I learned that in writing a book I gave up some of my privacy. When I share my thoughts with a friend in conversation or with a group in a lecture, I know at least vaguely those whom I am admitting into my thoughts and life. But strangers would buy the book! At least that was the hope!

On this my 40th birthday, I know I've also learned something because I've chosen a way of life in which I won't have a child. I always think of a son. I can't imagine what it is to be a little girl growing up. But I can vaguely remember what it was like to be a little boy growing up. I suspect mothers are better at allowing their sons to grow to manhood and fathers are better at allowing their daughters to grow to womanhood than either is at watching non-manipulatively the growth of the offspring of their own sex. I'll bet dads, through their sons, want to redo a lot of their own growing and mothers the same with their daughters.

I've watched boys and girls grow, and young men and young women; but they were not my own sons or daughters. I sometimes had a hand in their growing, but they were never mine and I was never theirs. I saw myself at times in their growing up—at least I thought I could remember going through what they were going through. But since they were not my offspring, I suspect I was less tempted to redo my own growing up in them. And from that I think I learned something.

And today I'm 40. Some speak to me out of a sense of pity, presuming this is traumatic for me. It's not. Others speak words of encouragement—presuming, I suppose, that aging is discouraging to me. Not yet. I'm glad to arrive at this milestone of life, not because it seems like an accomplishment, any more than youth seems like a virtue, but because it makes me grateful for my life—my youth and my aging. I planted my tree. It died. But it did something for me. I wrote my book. I hope it continues to sell. It did something for me. And I am living celibacy. I intend to continue. It has shaped my whole life and my feelings and attitudes toward trees and books and other people's children. And for this I'm very grateful.

KEITH CLARK, *Capuchin*

Where I Come From

Celibacy, as an option for me, began with my father. He loved me. I think he bought me my first and only electric train a couple of months before I was born. He and Mom thought for some reason that I was going to be a girl, so they planned to name me Mary Jane after their best friend. But boy or girl, I was going to have an electric train.

My mother loved me too. She was such a tiny woman that she wasn't supposed to be able to have any children. But when she found out she was pregnant, she was so happy she couldn't even wait to tell Dad first. On her way from the doctor's office to the ballpark where Dad was playing on the local team, she met another family friend and told him first. I saw Harold today as I was having coffee with my dad at a local coffee shop. I didn't speak to him, but I wanted to ask him if he knew that except for my mother and the doctor he was the first one to know about me. Years later Mom told me, "I wanted to tell everyone that there was going to be a you!"

My mother cried the first time she saw me. "You were so tiny, and I like my men tall!" she told me later.

When they brought me for baptism, Dad told Father Mc-Collow, "His name is Donald Michael Clark, and we're going to call him Mickey." It wasn't until I was in eighth grade that I even knew my first name was Donald. (Keith is my community name.)

For years I thought I knew why Dad had given me his

first name but a different middle name by which I was always known. Last year I asked him, though, just because I wanted to hear it from him. I was right: He wanted me named after him because I was his firstborn, but he didn't want me to be called "Junior."

Over the years of growing up I disappointed Dad a lot. But I made him proud too. Dad had been a basketball star in high school. I grew up to be as tall as he is, but I just didn't do well at basketball. And I did a lot of things he didn't like. And he told me about them. But he also told me when I did things he thought were good.

In eighth grade I told Mom and Dad that I thought I wanted to go to the seminary. They didn't say a word. I couldn't tell if they liked the idea or not. It was never mentioned again until after I graduated from eighth grade. I came home one afternoon during the summer, and as I threw my baseball mitt on the dining-room table, I said, "Hey Mom, I really think I'd like to be a priest." She stopped ironing and told me that after I had first mentioned the idea a few months earlier, she and Dad had gone over to talk to Father Mac about it. They had learned from him that there were three seminaries in the area, and the only thing they had been waiting for was to hear me mention it again.

I was whisked off to one of the seminaries by Father Mac. I took out an application, completed it and sent it back. Dad had made some financial arrangements so he could afford to send me.

Within the next couple of weeks, a salesman stopped in the store where Dad worked, and Dad told him that I was going to the seminary. The salesman mentioned that there was a seminary near Fond du Lac, Wisconsin, that prepared young men to be diocesan or religious priests. For some reason, the whole family drove to Saint Lawrence Seminary the following Sunday. The seminary was run by the Capuchins, and I met my first Capuchin that day: I thought he was funny-looking. However, at the end of our tour of the seminary the rector gave me an application form, and as we got back into the old wooden-bodied station wagon, Dad said, "Well, Mick, what do you think?" "That's the place," I said.

And that was the place where I spent four years of high school and one year of college. By Thanksgiving vacation of my freshman year of college I had decided, much to my own surprise, that I wanted to be a Capuchin rather than a diocesan priest. At Christmastime I told my folks, then my pastor.

Dad wasn't at all sure he liked the idea. And eventually he told me why. "Are you joining the Capuchins to escape the responsibility that goes with being a priest like Father Mc-Collow? Like running a parish?" I didn't know what Mom thought about it. And all Father Mac said was, "Good for you, Mick. I should have been a monk!"

Capuchins weren't monks, and I figured Father Mac had done all right being our pastor. I wrote something on the application for admission to the novitiate which was designed more to gain acceptance than to reflect my motivation, and in September of 1958 I was given the Capuchin habit at Sacred Heart Friary in Baraga, Michigan.

It was a cold, miserable day, misting and damp, when I was invested. I remember seeing Mom when she arrived; she was wearing a black dress instead of the orange one I had expected. I asked her after the investiture ceremony if she thought she was coming to my funeral or something!

Years passed. Mom's emphysema grew worse and she became an invalid. But the family—Mom and Dad and my three younger brothers—came to visit me at Baraga, then at Crown Point, Indiana, where I went after novitiate to finish college. In 1962 I moved with the rest of my class to Marathon, Wisconsin, to study theology. In September of that year I was going to make my final solemn commitment to the Capuchin way of life.

Mom's health had gotten worse and worse, and as she needed more care Dad gradually dropped his involvement in all the organizations he belonged to in order to care for her. My youngest brother, Charlie, learned how to run all the oxygen and other machines Mom needed intermittently. He, too, stuck pretty close to home after school, so he could be of help to her.

So it was, that on the day before I made my final lifelong commitment to a celibate way of life, I received this letter from my mother:

Dear Keith,

The folks will be getting there before my letter if I don't have it mailed by five. Tom does not work Friday so they will leave as soon after the noon hour as Dad can get away. They will see you early evening, we hope.

I'm still not too perky. Have pain in my side but not constant. It was bad on Monday so Dr. Murray came that night. He feels sure it is pleurisy, and you undoubtedly remember that is painful. It hasn't helped my breathing but the doctor upped my cortisone to four a day for two days and then I gradually cut down to what I was taking, about one and a half a day. I hope I'm feeling better before Dad leaves Auntie Dell and me, two old ladies, alone. And I should improve in two days.

We were all surprised that there are only four to make their solemn profession. You will have to explain again what happened to all. I know some are still a year behind at Crown Point, but four seemed so few left out of 30 (?) at Baraga.

I wanted to write something special for this day but it is not easy to express. It means so much to me, it is hard to understand why I cannot be there. So many thoughts in my mind—the day we left you at the door of Saint Lawrence, the year of wondering if you were staying because you really wanted to or because you thought we might expect it of you; how much easier it was the next years knowing you looked forward to going back and were really happy there. The shock of your wanting to join the Capuchins. It seemed as though we were really losing you. I'm sure I wasn't the only mother with a sad heart the day of investiture. But our visit at Baraga and our visits at St. Mary's were the most pleasant days of these past years. They did me so much good. There was so much happiness there. And when I was about to have surgery, even though I felt it shouldn't be, I had faith that the Capuchin prayers for me would be heard. And they were. So your final step to your way of life is not a sad one anymore.

I am glad you found this way. I only wish I could share the day with you, which is just selfishness. I hope Father Mc-Collow will be able to go but he seemed to feel that Saturday was too difficult a day to get away. He will bring Communion if he doesn't go, and Father Kunz will bring Communion if Father Mac finds he can make the trip.

And my Communion and prayers will be for you especially as they have been so many times. So many devout Catholic mothers would so like to have a son become a priest. I could never understand why I was so blessed. It is a great privilege God has given us.

Tom and John are to go to Grandma's for supper so I must see about mailing this before they all disappear, if they haven't already.

Much love,

Mom

Later that year my youngest brother said he wanted to go to Saint Lawrence Seminary, too. My brother John was already there, and was planning to join the Capuchins. Mom found it so very hard to see Charlie leave home. It was perhaps the biggest struggle of her life. One day she wrote to me: "That is something mothers have to learn—to let their children go. And probably only a mother fully understands."

Charlie did go to the seminary; John did join the Capuchin Order, and Mom began to get worse. People would say that they hoped she would live to see me ordained. But I never heard Mom ask for that; she wanted to live only as long as Charlie needed a mother. A little more than a week before she died, she wrote. Her biggest worry was that she might be putting expectations on her sons to be more than they might feel they could be or wanted to be.

Dad took Mom's death hard but well. During the next

two years he had a bit of a hard time letting me grow up. I was, after all, his child. I told him one night that I could remember him when he was the age I was now. And he said, "Yeh, I guess you're right." And I could grow up.

I had parents who loved me, but who didn't cling to me. When I met men at the seminary who seemed to make that "love-but-don't-cling" their way of life, I was attracted to them. They too loved me at some real cost to themselves, but never clung to me or tried to get me to cling to them. I opted for celibacy in their brotherhood, I believe, largely because I was prepared to see the beauty of it by my father and mother.

I know that every thought I have about celibacy is colored by the fact that I come out of this background; so are the observations, reflections and opinions in this book. Since other people see things in the perspective of their own backgrounds, I thought it might be good to let you know where I come from.

And I'd like to say a word about where I'm going in the pages which follow. It wasn't until a friend asked me, "For whom are you writing?" that I realized I was addressing married and single people as well as those who live a commitment to the celibate life. I am writing for celibate people and their friends.

Many of the things I want to share in this book apply to human life. I will be applying those human realities to the living of the celibate life, but I don't mean to imply that they are true exclusively of a celibate life. I cannot speak from experience of their application to married life; I will be speaking only of what I know from experience.

♣ *Part One*

Observations

♣ Chapter One

There Are Those Moments

In my lifetime I have experienced moments of intimacy and moments of loneliness. I have reflected on them a lot, especially late at night when I am alone in my room. My reflections have led me to think about the moments immediately preceding and following my birth. I have wondered from time to time if these moments are not, perhaps, the epitome of life's physical and emotional experiences of intimacy and loneliness.

Loneliness and intimacy are spiritual experiences; but they are spiritual experiences which are open to me only because I have a body. It strikes me that when I was fully formed in my mother's womb, my feeling of being at one with her must have been intense. I could not reflect on that experience then; but I was already me, and I was related to another person in a kind of oneness of life which may be a model of intimacy. It also strikes me that the moment I was forced from that essential physical and emotional oneness with my mother into an outside world may epitomize the separation from others which I perceive as the root of loneliness.

I arrive at this reflection because once I counselled a young man who clearly remembered the physical and emotional experience of being born. He didn't identify it as a description of being born, but he told of an emotional experience of being surrounded by a warmth and security which sustained him, and of the sudden lurching sensation—"Like I was in a car accident and was thrown from the car"—which threw him into a bright and cold frightening emptiness. I felt sure he had gotten in touch with an emotional memory of birth which is indelibly inscribed in his psyche. Further conversations over several years convinced me that this young man has experienced a very incomplete infantile amnesia—that permanent and normally complete repression of our earliest childhood memories from our consciousness into our unconscious mind. Whether or not that is true, his experience of remembering *something* on the physical and emotional level has invited me to reflect on the moments immediately preceding and following birth, and to think of them as the epitome of life's experiences of intimacy and loneliness.

It's not too often that I think about what it must have been like to be born. But as I look back at the 40 intervening years, I recognize that my life has continued to have moments of intimacy and moments of loneliness. I have not found life to be lonely, nor have I found it to be intimate; but there are those moments . . . .

I have experienced other moments which can be characterized by differing ways of being involved with others; for example, hostility and alienation. They seem like less natural moments than loneliness and intimacy. Intimacy seems to me to be a moment of being with another and enjoying it; loneliness seems like a moment of being separated from others when I would like to be with them. Hostility and alienation seem like moments of being against others and in some way enjoying it, or of experiencing others being against me and not enjoying it. Loneliness and intimacy seem like unavoidable moments of life for normal people. Hostility and alienation seem like unnatural human experiences, even though we may experience them often in our lives.

I don't think of my life as neatly divided into moments of loneliness and moments of intimacy. I know only that such moments exist, and that they invite me to enter them, even to enter them fully. They are fleeting moments usually, but not less real because they are not permanent.

Until I reflected on the moments surrounding my birth as possibly representing my initial experiences of intimacy and loneliness, I thought that they were opposite ends of a spectrum. I no longer think of them that way. Hot and cold may be opposites in that way. Loneliness and intimacy are merely distinctive moments in the flow of life, one experience excluding the possibility of simultaneously experiencing the other. They are mutually exclusive, but not opposites.

I have found it difficult for most of my life not to judge the relative worth of loneliness and intimacy. From my birth I have experienced intimacy as pleasant on the physical and emotional level, and loneliness as unpleasant. From the perspective of my own comfort, it is tempting to judge loneliness as bad and intimacy as good.

But one March evening several years ago I was able for the first time to say that loneliness was valuable, and mean it. And with that began an articulation of the meaning of celibacy which I have found to be somewhat satisfying.

Most of the details of that evening are blurred now, but I can still remember impressions which those forgotten details made. I had been invited by five men, who were about to be ordained deacons, to join them in an A-frame cabin in the Wisconsin woods. One of the deacons-to-be, Paul, was a dear friend whom I respected and admired greatly. I hardly knew the other four. But they received and accepted me—which I took to be a tribute to their trust in Paul who had invited me. As our evening together began, I had one thing in common with the four: trust in Paul.

The evening began with Eucharist. The readings were from Jeremiah and Luke. I don't even remember what the readings were, but they spoke to me strongly of the need to sink roots into soil near the stream in order to have life. I suggested, hesitantly at first, that the liturgy called us to loneliness—not simply to alone-ness, but to loneliness. To be alone to the point of experiencing our separateness is necessary if we are to "get off stage," I told them. And in my heart I was telling myself that everything and everybody will disappoint, not because things or people are bad, but because I yearn for more than anything or anybody can give me.

I found myself really believing for the first time that loneliness was good, even necessary. I still have some notes I wrote when I returned home late that night. I was surprised at the experience, and at some of the things I had said with such conviction. I didn't really know their source inside of me. I knew there was irony in the scene which took place in that A-frame in a Wisconsin woods: There I was, speaking with conviction about the need for loneliness and for being off-stage, and I had been put on stage by a brother whom I loved so tenderly and closely. I knew the young men were about to make a commitment to a celibate way of life as part of their commitment to ministry. And somehow I knew that the commitment to a celibate way of life required more than the negative view of loneliness arising from its physical and emotional effects. I believed the words I spoke; but I also knew of my own need for being "on stage" and my need for relatedness.

Whatever it was that was going on inside of me that evening, the conversation in the A-frame stimulated a desire to understand the human experiences which underlie the value of celibacy in a person's life—in *my* life. The years since have seen several of my closest friends—men with whom I shared much of my life—opt to leave their celibate commitment. This has been a further impetus to me to try to articulate for myself the human experiences of intimacy and loneliness.

As I have reflected these past years on the experience of intimacy and loneliness, I have found that understanding these moments better has led me to appreciate the possibility and beauty of the human lifestyles of marriage and celibacy. Like moments of intimacy and loneliness, like the moments immediately preceding and following my birth, celibacy and marriage are opposites only as ways of life which mutually exclude one another, not as opposite ends of a spectrum.

In reflecting on life's moments of intimacy, it seems to me that much of what passes for intimacy is not; and many of life's intimate moments are not recognized and celebrated as such. Intimacy is a human experience of being mutually transparent to another or with others in such a way that personalities are fused but not obliterated or lost in the other.

Intimacy and romance are often confused with each other. An intimate moment can be romantic; but it need not be. Let me share some experiences to illustrate what I mean.

It was a very intimate moment for me, and one which recapitulated a great many intimate moments over a seven-year period of my life, when I stood as celebrant of the liturgy in a chapel full of friends the last evening I was to live at Saint Felix Friary. I had been there for seven years. I knew the people who had gathered for the liturgy and the farewell party which followed. I knew their stories—those vagaries of life which had brought us into one another's lives. As each one came to receive Communion, I could recall the tragedies and joyous moments which had brought us together. They knew me. And they knew I knew them. I had planned to say some final words of thanks and some sentences which would sum up the past seven years. But at the end of the liturgy, when I tried to speak to those people whom I loved, I choked with emotion. All I could get out was the first sentence of my intended speech, "Thank you for allowing me into your lives." I was trying to fight back my tears, and they were holding back theirs. I still get choked up when I recall that evening. It was one of life's intimate moments; but it was not romantic.

I was involved in an intimate moment with Vince and Jody one spring evening when Jody suddenly left the dinner table at Saint Felix Friary where she was receptionist. Her husband, Vince, the cook at the friary, followed seconds later. It took several minutes before we noticed they were gone. I went looking for them and found them standing on the small rise at the edge of the woods. They were in each other's arms, and even from a distance I could see that they were crying and wiping each other's tears. As I walked up to them, they told me through their tears of a tragic event in their young married lives. They believed that Jody had a tubal pregnancy. They didn't know just what that meant or what options were open to them. They knew only that they were faced with what could be a life-or-death decision. They learned soon after that Jody was not pregnant. But that spring evening they were open to each other in their worst fears and in their bravest decisions. I experienced the intimacy I was witnessing with them and was included in their embrace on that little rise next to the woods. It was one of life's moments of intimacy—perhaps a moment of romantic intimacy for them. But I did not experience it as romantic.

Another intimate moment I remember occurred when two good friends met at a funeral home. Lucy was mourning the death of her husband and her friend was there to share her grief and offer support. The friend, a widow herself since the previous summer, greeted the family as she moved toward the coffin. After kneeling at the side of the coffin she then went to her friend and said, "Lucy, what would we do without our faith?" They cried in each other's arms, and knew that the loneliness caused by the death of their husbands was alleviated during the non-romantic intimacy of that brief moment.

Intimacy is what happens when two colleagues embrace as one is leaving for a new home hundreds of miles away after both have just finished the last detail of a project that has occupied their energies for three years.

Intimacy is what happens when a man in his early 20s finds the courage to share with a friend the fact that he is gay, and can tell by the friend's response that their friendship is real enough that he is accepted. At last he is able to share with someone the doubts and fears and struggle which made self-acceptance so difficult for many years.

Intimacy is what happens between a college sophomore girl and a junior boy as they kiss each other goodbye for the summer vacation, complete with promises to write daily while they are apart. It is one of life's moments of romantic intimacy.

Intimacy is what happens when the young bride invites her husband to enter her body to seal the pledge of their lives to each other which they made earlier that day. And intimacy is what happens 30 years later as the two lie together and recall their first night of marriage, looking back through the pains and joys of the intervening years. Both moments are romantic for them.

Life has moments of intimacy. Sometimes they are accompanied by great affection, sometimes not. Sometimes they are pleasant, sometimes sad. Sometimes they are sexual, sometimes not. Sometimes they are romantic, sometimes not. As often as two or more persons are intentionally transparent to one another in a way which brings their personalities together without obliterating any of them, there is intimacy. The moments come and go; the capacity for intimacy remains. Moments of intimacy are always satisfying in some way, but they are always incomplete. Even when they are very satisfying in the joy of the moment, they are incomplete in that the moment ends. Other concerns of life take each sharer of the intimacy into other pursuits with other people. But intimacy *is* one of life's moments.

Another kind of moment I have experienced and reflected on is loneliness. In my reflecting I have come to believe that it is important to distinguish moments of loneliness from moments of alienation and hostility. Loneliness will accompany those experiences at times, but loneliness is a different experience. I can feel very hostile and at the same time sense a companionship—an intimacy, if you wish—with others who are my allies in moving against a common enemy. I can feel alienated and know of my comradeship with men and women who are someway threatened by others. Loneliness is a more neutral and more natural experience than are hostility and alienation.

Loneliness is what happens to a 24-year-old religious brother who returns home from his last class before Christmas vacation and finds no mail in his mailbox. He doesn't feel as if people are moving against him, and he doesn't feel hostile. In itself, no mail two days before Christmas tends to produce loneliness in healthy people.

I experienced loneliness one Christmas when I sat alone in a local pancake house playing with the meal which was taking the place of Christmas dinner. My father was in a hospital hundreds of miles away and my mother was with him. All the religious brothers I lived with had gone to their families' homes for the day. I knew our family would be celebrating Christmas in February after Dad got out of the hospital. And somehow Christmas dinner at the pancake house was an experience of loneliness.

Loneliness is what happens to a young man after the ecstasy of the birth of his first daughter. He had been with his wife in the whole process of labor and delivery, spent the evening in her room with her, and celebrated the rest of the night with his parents and friends. He then returned to the empty house, and felt lonely. No alienation, no hostility; just loneliness.

Loneliness is what happens to a 38-year-old priest, a member of a religious community, when he arrives home after a week away and finds everyone is out for the evening or gone to bed. No alienation, no paranoia, no hostility, no self-doubt; just loneliness.

Loneliness is what happens to a happily married woman who lies awake beside her sleeping husband after a very satisfying moment of sexual intimacy. No fear, no self-doubt, no depression, no alienation, no hostility; just loneliness.

Loneliness is what happens to the keynote speaker at a

convention in a strange city when he or she leaves the podium and the social hour and goes to the hotel room. Well-received when speaking, that individual still experiences loneliness. No self-doubt, no alienation, no depression, no fear; just loneliness as he or she turns out the light.

Loneliness is what happens to me many nights when I close my door to get some privacy and time to pray, and I hear footsteps outside my door and want to open it and invite the passer-by in for a conversation. Instead I stay with my attempts at praying. I don't feel neglected; nor do I feel as if I am rejecting others. I know what I am about is worthwhile; but I still feel lonely.

Life has moments of loneliness. Sometimes we experience them in a crowd; sometimes when all alone. Sometimes those moments are deliberately chosen; sometimes they seem forced upon us. Loneliness can become unhealthy and even neurotic if it is not entered into in a healthy way, or if it is aggravated by fear, guilt, anxiety, depression, alienation, self-doubt or hostility. But in and of itself, loneliness is simply one of life's moments.

I sometimes think that life's moments of loneliness are seldom accepted and entered into as the uncomplicated moments they are. Loneliness is so often accompanied by self-doubt, depression, sadness, a sense of alienation or hostility, fear and anxiety, and these accompanying feelings color the experience with a negative hue. Focusing on these feelings which accompany loneliness may even obliterate our recognition of loneliness altogether. Or at the very least we may be inclined to worry about the fact that we are momentarily lonely.

After that evening with the five deacons-to-be in the A-frame in the Wisconsin woods, I began to recognize more clearly and to accept more fully life's moments of loneliness. And I began to examine more closely life's moments of intimacy. I don't know if those five men even remember the evening we spent together; I doubt if they remember anything I shared with them. But I can look back now and see that ever since that evening of liturgy and conversation, I have been more able to accept life as it happened to me—as I lived it. I can see that I began that evening to be willing to admit to myself that I was lonely at times. And I can see that I have looked more deeply at my experiences of being lonely and at my moments of intimacy. My life has many of both kinds of moments. Since I have begun to accept that fact, and not try to pursue and prolong moments of intimacy as desirable, and not try to avoid and escape moments of loneliness as bad, I have begun to further understand the lifestyles of marriage and celibacy.

♣ *Chapter Two*

Entering Those Moments

Moments of intimacy and moments of loneliness cannot be avoided. Trying to avoid them could drive us crazy, and it certainly would make us aloof from life. I feel invited to enter life's lonely and intimate moments. It is as if I belong to those moments and they belong to me because I was born. And yet I also experience a desire to protect myself from those moments. There is something fascinating but frightening about being confronted with one of life's moments of loneliness or intimacy.

As I think back on some of the intimate moments of my life, I know I was drawn to enter them, even to enter them fully; and I was frightened by the thought of allowing myself to get involved at all. I think again of the evening when I was about to leave Saint Felix Friary. I enjoyed that whole scene in the chapel and in the hall after the liturgy. And yet, as the moment approached and I was getting ready for the Mass, there was some part of me which just wanted to forget the whole thing. "Why even provide this occasion for all of us to get emotional over our impending separation?" I had asked myself all that day. But simply to pack my bags and leave without saying goodbye couldn't be the right thing to do. At the end of the liturgy I had wanted to reveal my heart to those people, but I resisted the invitation to do so fully. It would make me too vulnerable, I felt—too naked. If I could have simply said the words I wanted to say it would have been all right. But to become transparent to them to the extent of allowing them to see my tears—that I was not able to do.

The same fascination and fright seemed apparent to me in my walk across the front lawn to the rise where Vince and Jody stood in each other's arms. I wanted to join them; but I also knew fear in approaching them.

I've experienced the same thing in moments of romantic intimacy. A young lady, whom I find very attractive, stayed after Mass on Christmas morning. "I want to wish you a very special Merry Christmas," she said, "because you've helped me understand the meaning of the incarnation." She put her arms around my neck and I put mine around her waist. We kissed affectionately, and I was becoming sexually stimulated. I felt invited by this moment of romantic intimacy to enter ever more fully and more vulnerably. But I also experienced fear at the prospect of continuing to involve myself in the moment.

My fascination with life's moments of intimacy lets me know clearly that I have a need for intimacy. My hesitancy to enter these moments tells me that I also fear intimacy. My need for intimacy and yet my fear of it has been in me, I suppose, since somewhere in childhood or early adolescence. I can remember my grade-school romance with Donna. I wanted to get her attention, but when she looked at me I turned away and pretended even to myself that I wasn't interested. I can also remember the fascination of wanting to get involved in the roughhousing of the kids in our neighborhood, but not wanting to get so involved as to also get blamed for overturned garbage cans or broken windows. I have known a need for, and a fear of, both romantic and non-romantic intimacy for a long time.

I'm not sure if it is because of my need and my fear, or if it is only because of maturing along with them, that I became aware of my capacity for intimacy. And as it became more and more clear that I did have a capacity for intimacy whether I was experiencing my need for it or my fear of it, my needs and fears came more into perspective. And I learned that I could make choices about how to enter one of life's moments of intimacy whether or not I was experiencing a need to do so, whether or not I was afraid to do so. I discovered that the physical and emotional level that I experienced in my needs and fears was not the only level at which I could respond to one of life's moments of intimacy.

I have reflected more than once on how the need for physical and emotional intimacy is only part of the human experience. As I've watched people deal with meeting a friend's dog, I've learned something. At first meeting, both the animal and the person are suspicious, especially if the animal is a large one. In the course of an evening's conversation the person makes tentative attempts to relate to the dog, and unless the dog is very high-strung, it seems drawn to relate to the stranger. The outcome may be successful as the dog responds to the person's attempts to pet it. It may not end congenially. But there seems to be a need at our physical and emotional level—the level which we share with the animal world—to be known and accepted by another. It seems equally clear that the physical and emotional level does not exhaust the human person's capacity for intimacy.

Beyond the needs and fears which are activated at times, there is in mature humans an abiding capacity for intimacy and an ability to exercise that capacity to be intimate by free choice. Needs and fears can drive us to enter an intimate moment fully and vulnerably or to flee it altogether. By itself, our need for intimacy can drive us to intimate acts whether or not there is true intimacy. And our fear of intimacy can hold us back from expressing our oneness with other human beings. Our abiding capacity to choose if and how we will enter such moments frees us from absolute domination by our needs and fears. A mature person can enter a moment of intimacy as fully and vulnerably as the moment will allow and in the manner in which the moment invites.

I must admit it is tempting to try to draw a rather exact parallel between our needs and fears and capacity in regard to intimacy, and a similar set of needs and fears and capacities in regard to loneliness. But if there is such a parallel, I did not experience it in my growing up. Until that night in the A-frame, I don't think I experienced any fascination with loneliness. Nor do I remember before that night experiencing anything which I could call a capacity for loneliness. I knew moments of loneliness; but I feared and avoided them. I suspect that at my physical and emotional level—that level which was awake before I was born—there is very little that is inviting about loneliness. And I have a hunch that this is true because the experience of being born is etched into my emotional and physical memory as traumatic, much the way it is in the young man who in counseling could remember being born. For all of us, I imagine, there is an unconscious memory of the moments immediately preceding our birth and following it. And at the emotional and physical level it is probably impossible for any of us to choose the trauma of being separated from another when we remember the experience of being one with another.

As much as I tried in my growing up to avoid lonely moments, they were still there. At times I could distract myself from them by joining the group of friends I hung around with, or simply by listening to the adventures of the Lone Ranger on the radio. But at other times the crowd and the radio and the ordinary occupations and preoccupations of life could not distract me. I felt lonely, and I didn't like it.

As I grew older I began to see real value in being alone. It provided a chance for reflection and prayer. I liked to be alone with my thoughts sometimes. It gave me a sense that I was somebody even away from the crowd, and even when I wasn't doing something. Eventually I began to feel and to speak about the need to be alone, and when I wanted to be alone I would seek the opportunity. But being alone because we want to be isn't an experience of loneliness. Loneliness is being alone and knowing we are alone, but knowing we want to be with others.

It wasn't until that evening with the deacons-to-be that I

seriously entertained the notion of entering life's moments of loneliness. I would still try to be alone when I wanted to be, but I began to stay alone even when I did not want to be. And I discovered gradually that at a level beyond the physical and emotional there is an ability to respond to the invitation to enter life's moments of loneliness. That is the level of myself which recognizes that part of who I am is a person radically unique, incomplete, limited and separate from others. I think of this as the level of the "self," the truly personal level. It is at this level I realize no one and nothing can ever silence completely the self-doubt and neediness which are at my core and which come from an inner sense of being incomplete.

I began to *recognize* the arrival of a lonely moment when I closed the door of my room, spread the blanket on which I sit to pray and lighted my candle. Sometimes the preparations were inviting; it was good to be alone to reflect, to pray and even to write. But other nights as I began the customary ritual, there was another sentiment overriding my desire to be alone to pray; I wanted to be with someone, even to pray with someone. I knew the value of what I was preparing to do, but my mind was filled with thoughts of other things which seemed more inviting. But I was willing to *accept* the moment of loneliness.

As time passed I began to *welcome* the arrival of lonely moments. I came gradually to know that they revealed to me a truth about myself which I seldom came to know and experience consciously—which I *could* not know and experience fully in any way other than in a lonely moment: I am from my mother's womb, essentially and uniquely separate, incomplete, needy and alone.

I can still remember quite vividly my first terribly humiliating realization of my own almost desperate sense of neediness and incompleteness. I was sitting at my desk alone in my office, preparing for a meeting with our provincial council. I was part of its staff, and I was to make a report to the members at their meeting in a few days. As I sat there staring at the papers in front of me, I began to daydream. And a scenario took shape in my mind.

I imagined myself standing before the provincial council, there to receive a new assignment. I had completed my work as Director of Formation to my own satisfaction and it was time to be relieved of that position and to take up something new. I was questioned about my preferences; and all of us reflected on my abilities and limitations. Thankfully there were some tasks and jobs which suggested themselves! I would not be unemployed! I was then asked pointblank if I had any preferences among the jobs we had discussed. I searched my heart and found only one thing to say: "For God's sake, brothers, please give me a job, the successful doing of which will be of some importance in your eyes!"

"Why do you say that?" they asked.

"Because I feel I have done a good job at the tasks I have been assigned in the past; but I also feel that you do not see those jobs as all that important. *I* have believed in their importance; and I continue to believe in their importance. But does anyone else?"

The scene faded amid mild protestations that my significant contribution to the province was not doubted. But those seemed like shallow words to me. And I emerged from my daydream again staring at the papers on my desk.

I'm sure the reason I remember that daydream so well is that it embarrassed me tremendously. As I went about preparing the report, I hoped fondly that the scenario would never be played out. If my primary consideration in asking for an assignment was its significance in the eyes of others, I would know of the shallowness of my life. But the fact that I had created the scenario in my mind told me of my need for the approval of others and their acceptance. And as I sat there and allowed the need to deepen until I felt it at my very heart, I knew that however embarrassing it was to face the depth of my need, it was so much a part of me that I could never be rid of it. I knew that morning in my office that no one could ever speak a word powerful enough to silence forever the doubt at the center of me—doubt about my worth and the meaning of my life, about my connectedness to others and the possibility of being dismissed and thrown away, doubts about my limitations and my incompleteness.

This sense of neediness and incompleteness experienced *at the level of self* enhances the need for intimacy as I experience it *on the physical and emotional level.* This realization on the level of self that I am essentially and uniquely separate, incomplete, limited, needy and alone makes the need for intimacy *personal* and *spiritual,* not simply emotional and physical. This *personal* sense of incompleteness also makes me want not to be distracted from contact with myself; not to have that sense of a unique, separate, limited and incomplete self laid aside or destroyed by coming together with another. If I contact this personal sense of self as totally unique and incomplete, there is something at the level of my need which impels me toward intimacy or at least some acts of intimacy with others. But there is also something about the personal experience of loneliness which makes me want never to have my sense of unique self obliterated by coming together with others.

It is ironic, perhaps, that the personal sense of incompleteness, uniqueness and separateness which invites me to enter life's moments of loneliness is also the experience which makes a truly human moment of intimacy possible for me. Intimacy with another is possible not simply because each participant in a moment of intimacy has a need for fusion with another, but because each has a sense of his or her own uniqueness, separateness, limitedness and incompleteness, and is unwilling to have that sense obliterated by coming together with another. Unless this unwillingness is preserved, the coming together will end in domination and subjugation, or surrender and obliteration of the individual personalities; and that is not intimacy. True human intimacy is the fusion of personalities that still leaves all personalities intact. If in the privacy of my lonely moments I can remain in contact with my limited, unique, separate and incomplete self, I am prepared to enter into life's moments of intimacy.

If loneliness and intimacy remain an experience at the emotional and physical level only, for me they differ very little from my initial experiences in the moments surrounding my birth. As I mature, other parts or levels of me awaken. These too must be brought into my experience of intimacy and loneliness, or these experiences will not be fully human for me; they will remain cheap and maudlin, frightening and fascinating.

I am physical and emotional, and so I suspect that I will always respond to moments of loneliness and intimacy with my needs and fears, with fascination and fright. I can't see any reason to be ashamed of that. And on the level of my physical and emotional self, I suspect I will always be tempted to judge intimacy good and loneliness bad; at least I will experience intimacy as pleasant and loneliness as unpleasant. But there is more to me now that was not awake at the moment I first experienced intimacy and loneliness. And that needs to be brought into my experience of being with others and enjoying it; and being away from others and wanting to be with them.

I have caught myself often living out of my need for intimacy and my fear of loneliness. I suspect I will continue to recognize such motivations throughout my life. I think that much of my involvement with others in a helping and nurturing way is motivated by my need for intimacy. And I'm quite sure I do my praying late at night partly because by 11:30 there is no one else to talk to except God! While I do recognize my need for intimacy and my fear of loneliness, I also know that my life is richer because my needs and fears have not been my only level of operation. I have recognized in human life a capacity for entering into life's moments of intimacy despite my needs and fears. And I have recognized in human life a capacity for entering life's moments of loneliness. And I have experienced a freedom in choosing to enter both of those moments of life.

I don't like being too analytical and theoretical about something which is so personal and experiential. But my observations have made marriage and celibacy make more sense to me than they used to. Allow me to recapitulate those observations.

First, there *are* moments of intimacy and moments of loneliness; they are not the only moments in life, but they are some. Second, those moments invite me to enter them. Third, along with the invitation to enter life's moments of intimacy and loneliness there is a hesitation or a fear to do so; in either case there seems at first to be the chance that I could lose myself by entering the moment. And fourth, beyond the level of needs and fears, there is an abiding capacity for both intimacy and loneliness in each mature person, and because of that capacity we can enter into moments of intimacy and loneliness in a very personal and spiritual way. Finally, I think I have observed that on the personal and spiritual level of the "self," intimacy and loneliness are related to each other: As we come to grips with loneliness in our lives, we increasingly expand the possibility of entering moments of intimacy.

I think they are related in another way, too. I have noticed that people who have entered either moment fully and vulnerably, because they are committed to doing so, have found God concrete.

♣ Chapter Three

Finding God Concrete

That strange and rather cumbersome phrase, "finding God concrete," has haunted me ever since I received a letter a few years ago from a dear friend named Jan. She had left her religious community about two and a half years earlier, discouraged because she felt that she wasn't able to bring all of herself to that community. She is a vivacious woman—23 years old when she left religious life—who is described by herself and others as a free spirit. It wasn't the demands of religious community life which seemed to her to exclude much of who she knew herself to be. It was an attitude prevailing within her community which valued above most other considerations a certain propriety as determined by community leaders.

Jan comes from a very affectionate and spontaneous family whose deep Christian faith and Catholic loyalty have not in any way hampered their experience of being great human beings. The whole family—mother and dad, and Jan's six younger brothers and sisters—tend not to impose their wishes on one another or on anyone else. About all they ask of others is that they receive the same kind of non-imposing treatment from them. They are not the least bit aloof from others. On the contrary, they are inclined to help and cooperate wherever their help and cooperation are welcome. It's just that they tend not to butt in where they don't feel they are wanted.

I had first met Jan while she was still a religious. Her

father knew she was experiencing difficulties and suggested she get in touch with the new priest in town. Eventually she did, and we talked periodically over the next two years. And we gradually became very good friends.

During the second year of our occasional conversations it was becoming increasingly obvious to me that Jan was beginning to consider seriously leaving religious life. It was equally obvious that if she did, she was leaving a way of life in which, if she had experienced it differently, she knew she could have been at home. But her urge to go barefoot in the grass and to dance and sing and generally have a good time with people seemed to her to distinguish her too sharply from those in her community who were more established and in charge of the order. Besides these rather observable characteristics, she experienced a private and personal struggle with her sexual and affectional needs. Her great capacity for intimacy seemed to find no outlet in religious life as she was being asked to live it. She may have perceived wrongly what was being asked of her, but those were her perceptions.

Eventually our less frequent conversations centered around the question, "If I leave religious life, then what?" I remember well the conversation during which the question changed from, "*If* I leave religious life . . ." to "*When* I leave. . . ." Jan had not noticed the change in her own wording of the question, and she was surprised when I asked her if she had heard what she had said. But leave she did; and she had been working steadily at a job for two and a half years—along with doing lots of volunteer work such as planning and playing and singing for liturgies—when she wrote to me.

As I remember it she felt she was not yet adjusted to her new life of work and socializing. As a religious she had lived in an environment that provided time and encouragement for prayer and reflection. Now she found she didn't have the time she needed to nourish her spirit.

She wanted to meet the right guy and hoped to marry

and raise children. She still prayed a lot, she said, but she was very aware of her desire to share her mind and heart and body with somebody concrete, somebody not as abstract as God.

I don't know how I responded to Jan in my letter to her, but in my heart and in my green-book this is how I responded:

> I love that woman. If I did not believe in the kind of commitment I've made, I'd pursue her. I sense in her a struggle with what she is to do with her life, and I feel so deeply the pain of that struggle.
>
> I want to say tender and profound things to her. I want to say, "Be true to *all* of your desires, not only to some of them." I want to say, "Do you want to sacrifice the breadth and scope of your horizons to attain the depth which part of you looks for in a concrete relationship?" I want to encourage her not to be seduced into marriage, but to remain still and incomplete until she knows the man she is to marry, or the life she is meant to live alone. And I want God to lead her to a religious community which could accept her being "horny" as a beautiful part of life which points up clearly the loneliness of life in which *God* can be found "concrete."
>
> But, God, you may know otherwise what is best for Jan. I know of my affection for her which makes me want to have her for my own; and I know of my love for her which makes me leave her alone and free from me. And I know and even feel the love *you* have for her—a love of which mine is the poorest distorted shadow. I rejoice in your love for her. You will lead her; I believe that. And I thank you that I can believe that.

Since that March—just about the time I was with the deacons-to-be in the A-frame—I have often used the phrase "to find God concrete." And it is almost as often met by puzzled looks, an outright question: "What do you mean by that?" or a correction from some people who know English grammar well enough to presume I mean "find God concretely." The puzzled looks and the questioning have urged me on to try to articulate more clearly what I mean. My inability to explain satisfactorily even caused me to stop using the phrase for a while; but I picked it up again because it expressed something real for me and something which I couldn't say in any other way. With those who continue to correct my grammar I continue to insist that I do not mean to use the adverb "concretely" to modify the verb "find"; I mean to use the adjective "concrete" and I mean it to modify the noun "God." The reason for my insistence is what I've experienced personally and what I think I have observed in others.

Let me share some of this; then I'll attempt again to explain the elusive meaning of the phrase "to find God concrete."

I think back again to that morning in my office when I had my daydream about appearing before my superiors. As I emerged from my reverie, it was embarrassing to face my shallowness and neediness. Yet strangely, as I allowed my initial glimpse of my separateness, incompleteness and neediness to deepen to the point that I knew it was something at my center, I ceased to be discouraged and ashamed. This contact with my essential neediness led me to recognize and admit and eventually to embrace the sense of helplessness and worthlessness which is at my core. It brought me into contact with things true of me which I never would have chosen to look at. And having come to know that I have needs too profound for any human person to fulfill, I turned to my God, who has, I believe, made me this way. I could see clearly that I, who am meant to serve my brothers and sisters, really lived much of my life trying to win from them their esteem and appreciation. My need for appreciation and affection would remain, I knew; but I also knew that no amount of it would be enough to silence forever my craving for it. My need could, however, turn me to God at a depth of myself which I most likely would otherwise refuse to acknowledge and accept. But in that moment I knew he has acknowledged and accepted me there already.

My experience of finding God concrete is linked with entering fully and vulnerably into such moments of loneliness. But my entry has to be full enough to bring into the experience not just the emotion of feeling lonely, but also the almost contemplative and intuitive realization of my own incompleteness, separateness, limitedness and neediness. And I have to enter vulnerably—taking the chance that this lonely moment could overwhelm me and even destroy me. I have to look more deeply at just how true is my initial glimpse of my essentially incomplete, separate, limited and needy self.

It's hard to explain, and I feel as though I'm doing a poor job of it. But entering fully and vulnerably into one of life's moments of loneliness has for me the sense of standing naked before myself and before my God. It isn't the brazen nakedness of demanding to be accepted as I am, but a vulnerable nakedness of being open to accusation or hurt. It is the sense of embarrassment, confusion, vulnerability, of being out of control, lacking in understanding, and things like that. And yet it is not accompanied by fear or depression, disappointment or anger, denial or alienation, anxiety or even sadness. It's just a full and vulnerable sense of my own unique incompleteness, limitedness, separateness and neediness. And I face it, not bravely, but simply.

My experience of entering fully and vulnerably into one of life's moments of loneliness usually comes when I am alone at night in my room, where I've come to pray. I have a familiar routine. Lighting the candle and spreading the blanket on the floor usually bring a sense of anticipation of a basically pleasant but very ordinary experience ahead—praying and reflecting. I make myself available to God in my simple ritual.

On other nights, however, my sentiment is not anticipation at all; it is reluctance. I can now recognize the approach of one of life's lonely moments. I am alone because of my own choice, but I experience, rather than pleasure, a desire to be with someone else. I think of all the people immediately at hand with whom I could be. And I try to dismiss from my mind the thought of going to the recreation room or to someone else's door.

The approaching moment of loneliness is like a wall of dense fog which invites me to step within. As I approach the fog, I'm tempted by the thought that maybe some human friend will interrupt me before I step into the unknown meeting place. And I have to fight my own desire to be called back. It would be more pleasant to share this moment of trying to pray, I tell myself. I'm tempted to seek the company of another, knowing that God can be found there too, and to ignore the invitation I feel at present calling me to step into the fog. And I usually find myself taking quite a bit of time walking up and down, as it were, in front of the fog, not stepping into it, and yet not turning my back on it and seeking some other companionship. My thoughts are pulled by every sound of footsteps outside my door to retreat farther from the fog and postpone my entry into it.

Eventually I feel like I slip out of all protective covering and face the fog squarely. I always imagine it to be along the Milwaukee shore of Lake Michigan where I have often walked. I know the shoreline there. In some places there is sandy beach leading to the water. At other places there are rocks. At still other points along the shore there are cliffs and steep drop-offs. At one section city workers have piled an old broken cement sidewalk to arrest erosion. I face the fog, and I don't know what's beyond its outer edge—rock, a drop-off, sand, gravel, pebbles, a cliff? I know only that I am called to step into the fog without defense or protection.

If I do, where before I was preoccupied with enticing thoughts of other friends, now the sound of footsteps is a threat to what I've begun. Somehow simply allowing the fog to envelop me—to touch me—brings the sense that I am so essentially unique and alone, and that I am known precisely as I am. The sentences become incomplete; then words fail. Pretense is gone. The slightest accusation would assure conviction; the slightest wave of love is felt as fully as a naked person can feel the waves of a breeze pass from foot to forehead. I cannot speak about God or even to God. I am simply in his presence. And I know it is not by my design—I did, after all, resist the entire ordeal.

I am touched in every curve and contour of my being, permeated clear through by the fog. I have never yet found out what was beyond the outer edge of fog. I have never noticed rocks or cliffs or sand or pebbles. There is only the enveloping, sustaining fog. The outer edge is always so foreboding; but the inner region is sustaining.

I cannot find a word to describe the experience of God I find there, except to say that he can be found concrete.

If, on returning from the fog, some friend would want to speak to me of God and tell me who he is, I'd want to put my finger to my lips and with my eyes invite my friend to silence, as I was invited to silence one Sunday morning by the experience of emerging from a walk in the woods with Vince and Jody. We had gone to the woods so I could do a family portrait of them and their two children. Even as they posed for the camera, the affection of the four for one another was obvious. The parents' peace and happiness were obvious even on the film. As we walked back to where we had left the car, Sarah and Joey toddled on ahead of us, examining the wild flowers sparsely sprinkled in the underbrush. It was a touching and holy moment for me, and I wanted to speak to them of God and of his presence in their lives and of how I felt his presence when I was with them. But one does not speak of God to people who have entered life's moments of intimacy fully and vulnerably, any more than one speaks of God to those who have entered fully and vulnerably into life's moments of loneliness. Words intended to inform about who God is or how he is present in our lives are useless and unnecessary when people have found God concrete.

Oh, we can share with one another how we have experienced him. We can learn from each other and from great spiritual writers about his ways. We can be confirmed in what we know of him by what we hear and what we read. But we don't know him better for all our talk once we find him concrete. We may share our faith in him, but no one introduces the other to him.

One evening very late I chanced upon a father and his son sitting in a woods. The father was several years past 50; the son, just past 20. The father's heart was breaking. Nothing in his life was making any sense to him—his job, his family or the like. The son didn't understand either, but at his age, such a lack of understanding provided only adventure.

That night they shared their bottle of reasonably good wine and their burden and their adventure with me. The man shed tears and complained aloud to God in front of his son and me, his friend. He eventually smiled through his tears and thanked us both with a love for which he could not find words. This night he had found some relief. After half a year of seeking he had achieved some sense of God's presence. The son took him home, not knowing I suspect, the burden his father had experienced in the absence of God, or understanding the relief his father experienced in the fleeting sense of the presence of God. But he was able to rejoice in the joy his father felt.

One week later, the father again entered the same woods late at night. This time he chanced upon me. Again he bore the burden of not understanding the meaning of his world and sensing God's absence. And this night he found no relief before venturing home.

I have pondered the two chance meetings, and I am led to understand even a bit more clearly the meaning of "finding God concrete." God reveals himself to the seeking father one time in a sense of his presence, but again and often in the sense of his absence. Both experiences are revelations, for even in the sense of God's absence, the father knows the one whom his heart seeks.

I am not under the impression that life makes more sense

to those who have found God concrete. Like the father I encountered in the woods, people who know God can still be confused and uncertain about the meaning of life or the events of their personal lives. Like all people they will have periods of months or years when life seems meaningless. But for those who have entered fully and vulnerably into life's moments of intimacy or loneliness and have found God concrete there is a strength of faith to face life when it sometimes seems meaningless.

So, after all these words, what do I mean "to find God concrete"? I mean to experience him concretely, true; and that the experience of God is substantial for the one experiencing him. It is not only the *experience* which is substantial; it is *God* who is found to be substantial. "To find God concrete" means that the God who is experienced as substantial is known to be real, is known to be present.

I want to say that it is a non-mediated and contemplative experience of God, but that may be inaccurate. It seems to me that it is not so much an experience of God as is often the case in praying; it is somehow more direct. It is not so much the experience of being touched by God as it is of *God* touching me. I experience not the touch, but the God who is revealing himself in his touch.

My own experience of finding God concrete has come by entering fully and vulnerably into life's moments of loneliness. I have observed others who have found him concrete because they have entered fully and vulnerably into life's moments of intimacy. Before I discuss my observations on what is required to enter fully and vulnerably into those moments of life, I would like to share two sections from scripture which have spoken to me about finding God concrete by entering fully and vulnerably into life's moments of loneliness.

About four months ago I had had an extremely hectic day, and my attempt to pray that night was done out of a conviction that it was necessary and not because the idea was inviting. Earlier at evening prayer one of my brothers had prayed a passage from Psalm 73. I suppose because it had been such a hectic day, a line caught my attention: "When I am with you, the earth delights me not" (Ps 73:25).

I could say amen to that. As a memory it was so true, not as a current experience. And that saddened me. I realized that I hadn't taken any time for serious praying for over a week. I had been traveling, and I hadn't even unpacked my bible or my green-book—a sure sign that it was only as a memory that I could say yes to the psalmist's prayer.

I was grateful to God for the memory, at least, and for the invitation it extended to me that night to take some time for praying. I was not at my own house, so it took some time to find a candle. I found one and went through the customary ritual. In the house was a young man with whom I used to pray when we were stationed together. I was tempted to seek him out to pray with him that night. He was part of my memory of praying. With him I could sit and pray for an hour and never say a word except a brief concluding prayer. But I decided even he would probably be one too many for that occasion.

I was afraid that it would sound too forced and unreal, but I believed the words of the psalm could be put forward as an expression of the result of a celibate person's taking a chance on entering a moment of loneliness. Having entered and having found God concrete, it is true: "When I am with you, the earth delights me not." No matter how delightful some earthly aspect of a genuine Christian spiritual life might seem as we approach a moment of loneliness and experience an urge to flee it, if we give ourselves to that moment fully and vulnerably, even those earthly elements of friendship and intimacy seem no longer delightful. And yet these are elements of a genuine Christian spiritual life! They are not to be shunned as evil or unworthy. But when we accept the invitation to find God concrete by entering fully and vulnerably life's other kind of privileged moments, even things at the heart of Christian community life can be gracefully and graciously laid aside. This is not because they are unworthy, not even because they are less worthy, but because there is an invitation to something else which is not earthly. Jesus spoke the great commandment in two parts. They are to be observed together, but they can be experienced separately.

The other scripture passage which spoke to me about the experience of entering one of life's moments of loneliness was from the Book of the Prophet Jeremiah. I find that the letter Jeremiah wrote to the exiles in Babylon gives some expression to the experience. Since birth we have in a sense been exiles in a foreign land. At certain moments our loneliness, our separateness, our incompleteness seem to come upon us, and we have the exile experience.

Jeremiah wrote to the exiles:

> Thus says the LORD of hosts, the God of Israel, to all the exiles whom I exiled from Jerusalem to Babylon: Build houses to dwell in; plant gardens, and eat their fruits. Take wives and beget sons and daughters; find wives for your sons and give your daughters husbands, so that they may bear sons and daughters. There you must increase in number, not decrease. Promote the welfare of the city to which I have exiled you; pray for it to the LORD, for upon its welfare depends your own.
>
> Thus says the LORD: Only after seventy years have elapsed for Babylon will I visit you and fulfill for you my promise to bring you back to this place. For I know well the plans I have in mind for you, says the LORD, plans for your welfare, not for woe! Plans to give you a future full of hope. When you call me, when you go to pray to me, I will listen to you. When you look for me, you will find me. Yes, when you seek me with all your heart, you will find me with you, says the LORD (Jer 29:4-14a).

As a celibate man I don't know just what to do with the part of the letter which advises taking wives and having sons and daughters! But the rest of the letter speaks to me of the exile experience of being born. God says through Jeremiah, "When you call me, when you go to pray to me, I will listen to you. When you look for me, you will find me. Yes, when you seek me with all your heart, you will find me with you, says the LORD."

In some ways that expresses my experience of entering one of life's moments of loneliness and finding God concrete. If I allow myself to have the exile experience, I find that God is with me. But this happens only when I enter such lonely moments fully and vulnerably, when I seek him with all my heart, when I become aware of my own essential neediness, separateness and incompleteness. When I allow the exile experience which began at my birth to flood me, then I find God concrete.

♣ *Chapter Four*

Marriage and Celibacy

Throughout the history of humankind, several lifestyles have emerged. I must admit that I am still very hazy in my understanding of their development, but I have read enough to understand that three have lasted: marriage, celibate religious life, and the dedicated single life. Others have come and gone, while variations of those which have lasted and those which have passed continue to crop up periodically.

All three of these have taken various forms in different eras of human history and in different cultures. Sometimes marriage was monogamous, sometimes not. In some cultures it was permanent. Some societies permitted divorce. At varying times in different cultures the form of the single life and the celibate religious life have taken different shapes and have been regarded differently. Sometimes these ways of life were typified by hermits, and at other times by religious communities. Sometimes they were highly esteemed and at other times they were looked upon with suspicion.

I know three women who are single because they decided never to marry. I know a few men who have made the same choice. I know several widows and widowers who have committed themselves to remain such for the rest of their lives. It is true of me, and apparently true of many authors who write about these fundamental lasting lifestyles, that I know very little about such a life and understand very poorly the dynamics of that single state. I suspect that those who have embraced this lifestyle suffer still from our lack of knowledge and understanding.

Celibate religious life differs from the dedicated single life in a few aspects. For one thing, celibacy as a lifelong commitment grew out of religious convictions and spiritual inspirations. It developed as a way of living the three human attitudes we now call poverty, chastity and obedience. Father Adrian Van Kaam (*The Vowed Life*, Dimension Books) has helped me understand the development and the dynamics of the religious lifestyle.

Poverty, chaste love and obedience are necessary for every human being: poverty is that attitude which enables the wise selection and use of *things*; chaste love is that attitude toward *other human persons* which does not violate those persons in any way, but respects and nurtures their being and becoming; and obedience is that human and humanizing attitude by which people listen intently to the meaning of the *events* of history and of their personal lives with a readiness to respond humanly. Without these three attitudes no human life would be possible. We would misuse and abuse the things in our life-space; we would violate and obliterate one another in our attempts to come together; and we would be deaf to the meaning of events as they unfold or as we unfold them.

Some people in history took up an explicit and concentrated living of these human attitudes. They developed a celibate religious lifestyle and committed themselves to it for life.

I have lived this lifestyle in a community setting for the past 20-plus years. I know about it from experience and from experience shared by others. The development and dynamics of this way of living are understood to some significant degree by some of those who have embraced it. There is also some equally significant appreciation of this lifestyle by many who have chosen other ways of life.

Other people—the majority of them—have taken up

marriage. They have been attracted to another human being and have entered increasingly into an intimate relationship and made a commitment to establish a family unit.

While the married life is the life embraced by the great majority of human beings, I sometimes wonder whether or not the meaning of its development and the dynamics of its everyday unfolding are understood very well either by those who embrace it or by others. Indeed many do know and understand it but casual marriages and a high divorce rate suggest that we all could try to understand this lifestyle better.

I have never experienced married life. But I have been allowed the privilege of sharing deeply in the lives of those who were preparing for marriage and those who have successfully established a lasting relationship of reciprocal love and have established and maintained a sound family unit.

There are two other groups whose lives cannot be known and understood simply by understanding the three lifestyles I've been describing. Those are the people who are single but not committed to that form of life, and those who have embraced a celibate life for the purpose of ministry, not for the purpose of living explicitly the attitudes of poverty, chaste love and obedience. I'd like to say a word about each of these just to distinguish them from those we've been examining.

While similar in some respects to the dedicated single life and to the celibate religious life, the "unmarried" life remains open to the possibility of a commitment to marriage or to religious life. The unmarried man or woman is dedicated to all kinds of pursuits, perhaps, but he or she remains uncommitted to one of the basic lifestyles discussed.

Priests who have taken on a commitment to celibacy for the sake of ministry share many things in common with the single person and the celibate religious man or woman. But the purpose of their commitment to celibacy is different. I believe the celibacy they embrace is the same as that which religious undertake. But for the religious man or woman, celibacy gives shape to the life of bearing witness to the attitudes of poverty, chaste love and obedience. For the ordained clergy who embrace celibacy for the sake of the ministry, their celibate commitment gives shape to the ministry they offer the church and the world.

In the remaining chapters of this book I am going to be speaking primarily about celibacy as it is lived and experienced by religious and priests. I am a religious man—a member of a brotherhood—and I am also an ordained priest. I "committed" celibacy several years before I was called forward for ordination. But I suspect that my experience of a celibate life is not too different from the experience of a celibate life for a priest who is not a member of a religious community. I will be unable to speak much about the dedicated single life because of my lack of personal experience of that lifestyle and my very limited acquaintance with those who have chosen it. I will speak a bit more of the married life, not because I have any experience of it, but because I do have some acquaintance with people who are married, and because a celibate life is most often compared and contrasted with a married life. Indeed, many who have left celibate life have done so because of their perceptions of the beauty of married life.

I think marriage and celibacy are related to each other much the way intimacy and loneliness are related, or the way the moment preceding birth is related to the moment following birth. In all three of these related pairs, the parts can be contrasted with one another, can be compared one to the other, can be understood better in relationship to one another. But I don't think of marriage and celibacy as opposites any more than I think of the moments before and after my birth as opposites, or of intimacy and loneliness as opposites.

I think married people have a special relationship to life's moments of intimacy and celibate people have a special relationship to life's moments of loneliness. I do not, however, think that married life is intimate and celibate life is lonely. Both lives have moments of each. I do think of marriage as a commitment to *stand ready* to enter fully and vulnerably into life's moments of intimacy. I do think that celibacy includes a commitment to *stand ready* to enter fully and vulnerably into life's moments of loneliness. I don't think married life is a commitment to intimacy, nor that a celibate life is a commitment to loneliness. The commitment in both cases is to *stand ready* to enter fully and vulnerably that moment of life to which one is specially related by commitment.

I want very much to be understood as to what I am saying and what I am not saying. I am *not* saying that celibacy is lonely, nor that marriage is intimate. I am *not* saying that marriage has more intimate moments than celibacy, nor that celibacy has more lonely moments than marriage. I am *not* saying that marriage is a commitment to intimacy, nor that celibacy is a commitment to loneliness.

I *am* saying that when two people commit themselves to one another in marriage, they are committing themselves to *stand ready* to enter fully and vulnerably into life's moments of intimacy. And if they do, they can find God concrete. I *am* saying that when men and women commit themselves to a celibate life, they are committing themselves to *stand ready* to enter fully and vulnerably into life's moments of loneliness. And if they do, they can find God concrete.

Married people have a special relationship to intimacy because they make a commitment to enter life's moments of intimacy more completely, more vulnerably, than is possible for the non-married.

Celibate people have a special relationship to loneliness because they make a commitment to enter life's moments of loneliness more completely and more vulnerably than is possible for the non-celibate.

Maybe a married man or woman can enter as fully and vulnerably into one of life's lonely moments as a celibate man or woman can. But I don't think so. A husband and wife are committed to one another in such a way that when one is lonely it is always the other's concern. The spouse may not be able to alleviate the momentary loneliness, but the commitment to share intimately each other's lives means that even the lonely moment can and should be shared. And in their loneliness they can find God. If their marriage is what it is meant to be, it is *together* in their experiences of intimacy and loneliness that they will come to find God concrete.

As a celibate man I cannot enter as fully and vulnerably into life's moments of intimacy as Vince and Jody, or Jim and Eloise, or Don and Mary, or Tom and Ann, or my mother and father. My life may have as many moments of intimacy as theirs, but I don't believe I have ever experienced the depth of intimacy that they have. I have experienced intimate moments, and I have found God there. But I have not found him in intimate moments as concretely as I have found him in lonely moments.

In either case I think it is the *commitment to stand ready* which opens the moment of intimacy or the moment of loneliness to the possibility of finding God concrete. When we make a commitment to marriage, the celibate religious life or the dedicated single life, we have limited and defined our whole life. It is one thing to know how limited one is by birth and growth; it is another thing altogether to know we have limited ourselves by choice and commitment.

Two people who commit themselves to each other in a Christian marriage make a covenant to provide the opportunity for sexual, romantic intimacy to find its highest possible meaning; namely, discovering God concrete. Sexual and romantic intimacy which is not experienced as deeply personal, and even sacred, because there is a lack of fidelity, will eventually disappoint. But the *commitment to stand ready* to enter life's moments of intimacy in this sexual and romantic way assures that the moment of intimacy has meaning beyond itself and beyond the physical and emotional expression through which it is experienced.

The present moment of intimacy draws much of its meaning from the commitment of the two persons to be there for each other in the future. And this commitment gives the single moment of intimacy a meaning which transcends itself, the couple, the expression of intimacy.

Without such a permanent commitment, the moment of intimacy will lead inevitably to disappointment because it promises and signifies more than either person really meant to give. In this sense the intimate moment entered into romantically and genitally without commitment promises more than it can deliver.

I think there is a parallel in the experience of loneliness for the celibate. For the celibate man or woman, entry into a present moment of loneliness, fully and vulnerably, has meaning in itself. And the commitment to stand ready to enter each of life's lonely moments gives this single moment a meaning which goes beyond itself, beyond the one experiencing it, and beyond the experience of the moment.

The fact that marriage and celibacy are not always experienced this way does not persuade me that they are not meant to be this way.

I feel reasonably sure that both married and celibate people face a similar kind of difficulty in their commitments to stand ready to enter two of life's different moments. From time to time both recognize how their commitment has limited their options. The sense of being limited at all can cause resentment; but the resentment tends to increase when we look back and see that our options have been limited by the choices we have made.

"If I knew then what I know now, I never would have made this commitment" is a phrase I have heard from celibate and married people alike. It strikes me that every decision and commitment is, in the light of subsequent information and experience, ill-informed. That's just the way life is. Whether we would or would not "do it again" is hardly the point. The point is whether or not we are actively pursuing the fulfillment of the commitments we have made. When we begin to concentrate on what our life *isn't*, and neglect to reflect on and actively pursue what it *is*, trouble will almost certainly follow.

If we will look at our lives and recognize that the limitations resulting from our choices and commitments have also opened the possibility of greater depth, and if we will pursue that possibility instead of lamenting the limitations, resentment can turn to gratitude. As long as we remain uncommitted, it is true that a wider range of possibilities is open to us. But it isn't until we have committed our lives to marriage, celibate religious life, or a dedicated single life that we can begin to achieve the depth of life which is possible.

I think people committed to a celibate life sometimes look at those who are committed to marriage and see a beauty there that is lacking in their own lives. And I know the reverse is also true. But for those who remain committed to their own lifestyle and pursue its possibilities, such recognition of the beauty of the life they have not chosen leads to genuine appreciation. I recall a letter I received from Jody some time ago. She wrote about her and Vince's difficulties in dealing with some of the practicalities of their married life—especially the need for Vince to find another job. She said in closing, "What do couples do who don't have a Keith Clark to be with them through it all?" As I read her words, my heart said, "Please, Jody, once in a while think about what a Keith Clark would do without a Vince and a Jody."

As much as I have recognized in Vince and Jody's life a beauty which mine will never have, and as much as people like Jody and Vince may recognize in my life something which appeals to them, none of us could do what we do for the others without being committed to the life we have chosen.

I'm sure that at times in the life of every celibate man or woman and in the life of each married person, the only reason for continuing is the commitment to do so for life. Continually reflecting on the meaning of life is very important to me. But despite my best efforts at this reflecting and at this trying to articulate the meaning of celibacy for me here and now, I know there will come a day when celibacy will not make any sense to me at all. I would be presumptuous to think that at any given moment I should be able to think my way through life. At times I'll simply have to live life, and think about it later.

All of us, I believe, like to have life make sense to us. And we like to have that part of life which has become central to the rest of our activities have meaning at all times. But there are times when I cannot discover or articulate the meaning of my life. I will have to experience lack of meaning and inability to articulate before I can reflect on the experience of living through meaninglessness. But at the point that the life to which I have committed myself doesn't make sense, commitment had better have a lot of meaning. Making sense out of life is something we do with our intellectual powers; committing ourselves to a way of life is something we do with our wills.

♣ Chapter Five

Commitments Evolve

I was first introduced to the notion that commitments evolve through a letter from one of my brothers in religious life to our province at the time he was asking for a dispensation from his vows. In the letter he traced the evolution of his commitment to Capuchin religious life, beginning with his home life, his attraction to the seminary, his gradual acquaintance with the Capuchin friars, his entrance into the order, his simple profession, his final solemn commitment, and his eventual ordination to the priesthood and first assignments.

He then traced the evolution of his commitment to the person he was planning to marry: their first meeting; their getting to know one another; their growing friendship; their attempted separation when they thought their friendship was developing into something which they might not want; their relentless feelings of attraction, affection and love; their serious discussions about their options and the consequences; and finally, his realization that through it all a commitment had evolved. He intended to take up this new commitment, not because of any anger or disappointment with his previous commitment or with the friars of the province, but because something else good had happened to him.

The letter made perfectly good sense, but it angered and hurt me and made me feel guilty. Perhaps if I had written more when he was away at school, perhaps if I had paid more attention to him when he was home for the summers—perhaps, perhaps, perhaps. I didn't like it because it all sounded so inevitable.

But as the years passed and my hurt, guilt and disappointment subsided, I began to look more clearly at what he had been saying. And I can now say yes to his notion that commitments evolve. And the commitments to celibacy or to marriage evolve in the way my friend explained.

At first they evolve through random happenings we probably have no control over—even such circumstances as the family into which we were born and our earliest treatment as infants. As we grow into childhood, we are able to make choices, and we choose things out of no particular pattern. As we grow, we begin to make choices which are more deliberate as others teach us what is important and right and good. Our choices begin to fall into patterns, but the patterns are those we've been given, not ones we've decided to make our own. As we mature, we begin to recognize the patterns of our choices and to evaluate them critically. Eventually we choose not only specific actions, but patterns of acting in order to attain certain personal goals, including the way of life we wish to live. At some point we say a solemn yes to the commitment which has evolved. If it is a commitment to marriage or to celibacy, our solemn yes is to a permanent lifestyle and has consequences for our entire life.

I can trace this development in my own commitment to celibate religious life. I have heard others trace their commitment to each other in marriage. In some ways the wedding day or the day of final solemn commitment to religious life seems like the day on which a lifelong goal has been attained. The commitment evolved from that first chance meeting to the free and deliberate embracing of a lifestyle.

But the goal is entry into a lifelong commitment; it is the *beginning* of a committed life, not the fulfillment of it. And part of the commitment to a lifestyle is to keep other commitments from developing which are contrary to the one which has now become central to my life. Other commitments will evolve; but I must keep *contrary* commitments from evolving.

Having said a solemn yes to a lifestyle, we dare not think that the evolutionary process of that commitment has ceased. Things will happen to us; we will continue to make random choices; we will still make choices because of an already decided upon pattern. It becomes our responsibility to actively pursue that pattern of choices which will continue the evolution of our life choice.

This active care for the evolution of our life commitment must take place on all levels of life—our thinking, acting, choosing, understanding, reflecting, experiencing. Life commitments are not assented to once at the moment of our solemn yes and then expected to remain static. There needs to follow a deliberate and relaxed pursuit of the fulfillment of the commitment which was begun in early life through random happenings, was ordered into a pattern of choices, and eventually was assented to with solemn free choice.

During the past several years I have listened to a lot of religious men and women struggle with a decision whether or not to leave religious life. Frequently what has prompted the question has been the fact that they have fallen in love with someone. Often the question is posed in terms like these: "Should I ever have tried to live this way of life? Maybe it was a mistake in the first place. Maybe I was never really called to religious life. It certainly doesn't seem to be working out, at least not in the way I had anticipated. And now I have learned something about me which I didn't know when I made my commitment to this way of life."

Whenever I hear those kinds of questionings, I am reminded of a priest I know who always concludes his final session with couples about to be married with some rather startling words. "We'll see you in church on Saturday. And after that you won't even think of me again until 18 to 36 months have passed. Then you'll be back to tell me your marriage isn't working. Well, I'll tell you right now that your marriage isn't going to work." The couple's faces usually fall, and as they look at each other and then back at the priest, he continues, "No marriage I know of ever worked. Either two people put their hearts into making it work or it dies. So put your hearts into making what you say yes to on Saturday work."

Often the same situation is true of the religious man or woman who has reached the point of having to decide whether or not to remain in religious life. I think sometimes it has been true that a person should never have tried to make a commitment to celibate religious life. Some were talked into making the commitment after they had decided, either in novitiate or before final profession, not to make vows. Others feel they have to leave because of lack of support within their communities. And some have not taken sufficient charge of their lives and have let commitments evolve which are contrary to the one made on profession day. At that point a commitment has evolved which is incompatible with the one they had made earlier. They are faced with a choice between an unattractive commitment they feel still binds them in some way and a newly evolved commitment which seems to have so much more life and enthusiasm in it.

It is really true, I believe, that almost all previous decisions will eventually look as if they were made without sufficient information and understanding. But I do not believe that means that the previous decisions are no longer "valid." They were valid when we made them, and they remain valid. If the validity of past decisions can be challenged by subsequent information gained by experience, then any decision made now will lack validity as time passes and we gain new information.

I am no longer inclined to hassle and argue with religious who have arrived at the point of leaving religious life. Whatever the legal and moral implications in the theoretical order regarding their commitment to religious life, in the practical order there is often relatively little choice open to them but to pursue the newly evolved commitment. If, however, I have the opportunity to confront and challenge behaviors and attitudes in religious which seem naturally to lead to a decision to leave, I am inclined to do so.

Commitments evolve. Once they have grown to full stature they simply exist whether or not there has been a solemn yes spoken publicly. There is very little anyone can do about them at that point. We will occasionally see men and women committed to a fundamental lasting lifestyle displaying attitudes and behaviors which indicate the evolution of commitments contrary to the one they have already made. It is a service to help them recognize this immediately. Confrontation only at the point of crisis is usually too late.

Fidelity to the commitments I have made demands an ongoing reflection on the meaning of the actions and attitudes relating to my commitment. I have to actively pursue the fulfillment of my commitment by continually trying to articulate the meaning my life has now. Perceptions and ideas which supported my decision when I made it become less relevant with the passage of time. The reasons I articulated 20 years ago cannot support my living of the vows now. If I have not reflected continually on the meaning of my life as I have lived it, I will eventually find myself with an archaic articulation that will no longer support my commitment. The result will be a weakened commitment. And an examination undertaken at a crisis will be directed more by the crisis than by a desire to understand the celibate commitment. At a crisis, the examination may be undertaken to show why the celibate commitment *doesn't* make sense any longer.

Perhaps I'm naive, but I believe this also applies to diocesan priests. I think the principles apply equally to married couples. But in the remainder of this chapter and in the following two sections of the book, I will be looking principally at the dynamics of commitment and fidelity as they can be found in celibate religious life and will be writing from that perspective. And most often I will be comparing and contrasting the celibate commitment with a commitment to marriage, because in my experience and in my listening to other celibate men and women we tend to see these as the alternatives which, though mutually exclusive, are open to us.

Two recent days have been filled with speaking with men who are committed to a celibate life and who are currently in love with a woman. Both chose to speak to me about it; both have given me permission to write about it. I am very close to both of them, and I want both to remain in religious life.

In my listening to them and speaking with them, I found myself challenging and denying some assumptions they are making.

The first assumption is that falling in love means a celibate life is impossible for them, or that they are not called to a celibate life. I don't believe that. I believed my moral theology professor when 15 or more years ago he looked at our whole class and said, "Every one of you will eventually meet the right person and fall in love." I believe falling in love is normal and natural for everyone. It's part of our emotional and physical make-up as sexual beings.

Secondly, both men assume that if being in love were "bad" they would experience some undesirable consequences. In effect they would have a warning. But I don't accept that. I think that for healthy people, being in love is a good experience and will have only good consequences. So, since both of these men are healthy, it is foolish for them to expect a "bad" sign that might make them stop pursuing their romantic love. Celibate men are bound to experience the expanded energies, the new verve of life that follows falling in love.

The third assumption is this: Somewhere in the future there will be a big vocational decision to make. I believe the decision is with us daily in the little inch and quarter-inch decisions we make. We are always actively pursuing a celibate vocation by the little choices we make, or we are pursuing a married vocation by the little choices we make. Somewhere in the future lies the *realization* that we *have made* our decision regarding our vocation by the small choices we have already made.

I see marriage and celibacy as two fields divided by a stream and connected by a bridge. We opt for one field or the other, and we take daily non-crucial steps into that field. The decisions of each passing day bring us more deeply into the field we have chosen.

We may indeed make mistakes in our decisions. We can, for example, pursue a celibate commitment through sexual repression. That is a mistake and those steps will have to be retraced. But when a person is healthy, he or she can enter either field and begin the journey.

I think my two friends have retreated from the field of their journey. They have come back to the bridge. They want to be free of previous commitments whose validity they now suspect. They tentatively put one foot and then the other on the bridge and gingerly begin to find a path into the field which is marriage. They will not have some catastrophic experience that will convince them they should get back in their chosen field. They are healthy and they are wise and they are cautious; mistakes are not to be expected.

But they think they are still standing on the bridge while all the time they are advancing well into another lifestyle which is as beautiful as it is satisfying. Their mistake is in not exploring carefully and steadily the field in which they began their journey. If they can accept without difficulty the beginning of their new path, they can accept every step they take after that. And as long as they think they are still on the bridge, they can take that first step with impunity.

Why didn't someone tell them, I ask myself, that the experience of falling in love is part of the field of celibate life? Why didn't someone warn them that this is not to be confused with being back on the bridge? Why weren't they prepared to continue walking in that first field, recognizing that they have just met a temptation, not to something bad, but to something good and beautiful? They have earlier decided in which field they wish to walk; they have now only to continue walking.

All this is easy for me to say because I am not currently captivated by being in love; and it's hard for them to hear because they are.

Commitments evolve; and once we have said yes to a life commitment, we have pledged ourselves to take charge of the evolution.

♣ Part Two
Reflections

♣ Chapter Six

The Paschal Mystery

In the summer of 1968 I had the extreme good fortune to be one of about 120 students taking a course in the theology of St. Paul from Father David Stanley, S.J. Perhaps I would exaggerate if I said that this final summer course on my way to a master's degree in Fordham University's Religious Education Department changed my life. But it certainly changed my thinking about life. It was Father Stanley who made the paschal mystery come alive for me. While I gladly acknowledge my indebtedness and gratitude to him for what he taught, I do not intend to hold him responsible for what I heard and have remembered of his lectures.

My understanding of the theology of the paschal mystery has brought some sense and continuity to my celibate commitment. I suspect that most of what I write in the rest of this book comes from this perspective of the paschal mystery. And I suspect it will be better understood if I share my understanding of this central mystery of our Christian faith.

I like best the articulation of the mystery as it is in Paul's letter to the Christians at Philippi. The hymn in chapter two expresses three movements in the mystery of Christ's life:

Though he was in the form of God,
  he did not deem equality with God
  something to be grasped at.
Rather, he emptied himself
  and took the form of a slave,
  being born in the likeness of men.

He was known to be of human estate,
   and it was thus that he humbled himself,
   obediently accepting even death,
   death on a cross!
Because of this,
   God highly exalted him
   and bestowed on him the name
   above every other name,
So that at Jesus' name
   every knee must bend
   in the heavens, on the earth,
   and under the earth,
   and every tongue proclaim
   to the glory of God the Father:
   JESUS CHRIST IS LORD! (Phil 2:6-11).

The first movement of the paschal mystery—he did not cling to equality with God, but emptied himself, taking the form of a slave, becoming what all people are; he was known to be of human estate—is downward from a position of separation and distance from our human condition to one of complete immersion in it. *Jesus, the Son of God, became what all of us are.* The gospels are full of evidence about how fully he became one of us. He took on our emotions as well as the limitations of our thought and expression. He had a human mind which had to be taught like all human minds. He had a human will by which he made human choices in accord with his Father's will. He loved as humans do, even to the point of having special friends within his band of followers and special friends to whose homes he could escape from his band of followers.

He did not cease to be God in this downward movement. But while remaining who and what he was, he became what all people are. The only limitation of humankind that he didn't experience was that of having sinned.

It stands as vivid testimony to the depth of the mystery of the incarnation that theologians have ranged from a minimal acceptance of Jesus' human nature—making it seem easier for him to be human than it is for us because he was sort of masquerading as a human being—to an acknowledgment of his human condition that is exaggerated to the point of attributing to him our human propensity for sinning. Our scriptures and our tradition tell us only that he was like us in all things but sin. We are even told that he was tempted *in every way we are* but he did not sin.

The second movement of the paschal mystery is again downward. The first is a movement down to our level; the second movement is to below the level we are usually willing to accept. As one of us he was humbler still, even to accepting death, death on a cross.

Death is a strange thing with us. We fear it, for the most part; we generally avoid the subject; we try to cope with it when we have to. For most of our lifetime we think of it in medical terms—the cessation of our pulmonary functions and our brain waves. As we or someone we love approaches death, we tend to think of it in religious terms—the person in his or her soul leaves the body and goes to God.

When the New Testament authors write of the death of Jesus, they are not dealing primarily with the medical or our Western religious concept of death. Had these been uppermost in the evangelists' minds, I think they would have had to reveal that interest in some way as they told of the raising of Lazarus and the daughter of Jairus. But it is only more recent theologians, doctors and religious believers who have wondered what kind of story Lazarus must have told at the supper table or what must have been the condition of his arteries and brain tissue.

When the New Testament writers speak of the death of Jesus, they always speak of it as his glorification. In the evangelists' accounts we frequently hear Jesus speak of his "hour," the "hour when the Son of Man will be glorified." St. John is the most explicit in developing what all the evangelists proclaimed; namely, that the death of Jesus was not the defeat his enemies had planned, but his victory over those who had made themselves his enemies, his victory over sin and over death itself.

St. John records at the very beginning of his account of the good news about Jesus that there is one who will come after John the Baptizer "who will baptize with the Holy Spirit." Later in chapter seven, John makes a parenthetical remark after Jesus says:

> "If anyone thirsts, let him come to me;
> let him drink who believes in me.
> Scripture has it:
> 'From within him rivers of living water shall flow.' "

John immediately adds: "(Here he was referring to the Spirit, whom those that came to believe in him were to receive. There was, of course, no Spirit as yet, since Jesus had not yet been glorified)" (Jn 7:37-39).

In chapter twelve John records the incident of the woman anointing Jesus at the supper table. The fragrance from the broken jar of ointment filled the whole house. In much the same images, John records the final words and death of Jesus: "When Jesus took the wine, he said, 'Now it is accomplished.' Then he bowed his head, and handed over his Spirit."

Much as the fragrance of the ointment from the broken jar had filled the whole house, Jesus' Spirit, with which he had come to baptize, was released to fill the whole church. The work he had been sent to do, baptize with the Holy Spirit, was accomplished in his glorification. In his death, Jesus shed the limitations that were part of his earthly experience, and once those limitations were shed, the Spirit was released.

I have an image for all this which is not very theological. It comes from an old Abbott and Costello movie, I believe. Through some fantastic means the two of them had become ghosts and could not be seen. In order to make themselves known they put on clothes made of ordinary materials. Because they were ghosts they could pass through walls and floors without difficulty. However, when they tried it with their non-ghostly outfits, the clothing simply fell in a heap on the floor as they passed through the wall. I sometimes imagine that in his experience of death, Jesus passed downward through the floor and left behind all those limitations which were part of his human condition. He still remained human like us, but because he accepted even death he shed the limitations which are part of our human condition in this life.

Paul takes up the evangelists' theme when he asks, "Do you not realize that we who have been baptized into Christ Jesus, have been baptized into his death?" By our baptism we are committed to a life of shedding our human limitations of sin and selfishness. Father Stanley didn't do any exhorting during that summer course. But one of the most powerful sermons I ever heard was his commentary on Paul's words, ". . . since one died for all, all died. He died for all so that those who live might live no longer for themselves, but for him who for their sakes died and was raised up" (2 Cor 5:14-15). Father Stanley looked up at us and said, "What that means is that nothing is so totally incompatible with Christianity as doing something selfish."

The death of Jesus, then, is his shedding of his human limitations without ceasing to be human. This is the second movement of the mystery of Christ.

The third movement is upward—Jesus' return to his Father. He returns as one of us, though he never ceased being God. Now, freed of human limitations, he is raised high and given, even in his humanity, the name which is above every other name—"Lord."

If the interests of later theologians have shaped a popular understanding of Jesus' death, those interests have even more fully shaped our understanding of Jesus' being raised to new life. I'll try to avoid the disputes surrounding a theology of

Jesus' resurrection. I simply believe in the bodily resurrection of Jesus, not because I believe the observable historical facts are the heart of the revelation, but because I find it too difficult to believe that those to whom the mystery was revealed could have grasped that mystery any other way.

The resurrection is not meant to prove something to those who would otherwise refuse to believe. If it were meant to prove something, it would seem to have been rather poorly handled! If he had appeared to Pilate as he ate breakfast that first day of the week, that would have proved something! No one saw him rise—a definite oversight if one were trying to prove something. And Jesus didn't appear to the crowds of people who were available. If he had wished to prove something, a public appearance would seem to have been in order. Interestingly enough, the New Testament writers speak of Jesus' resurrection as the work of his Father, not as an accomplishment of his own. We are told over and over that "God raised him" and that "he was raised." The resurrection was not a show of strength on Jesus' part to prove something to non-believers.

The post-resurrection appearances of Jesus were meant to reveal something to those who were prepared by their earthly experiences of him before his death to believe in him. In raising Jesus from the dead and having him appear to the disciples, God continued the revelation of himself which he had begun when he sent his Son into this world.

What, then, do the post-resurrection appearances of Jesus reveal? First of all, they reveal that he who had become what all of us are, and who had accepted even death, was alive! It is an article of the Christian creed that he died. How dead was he? He was buried! And this was not just a charade, a pretending to be dead. He actually died, but now he is alive!

Secondly, by appearing to his disciples after his resurrection, Jesus revealed that he is alive in a new and mysterious way. Something is always eerie about his presence after his resurrection. The old familiarity is gone. Often, after his resurrection, the disciples fail to recognize him immediately. Or they know it is the Lord, but they are afraid to say anything to him. It is definitely the same Jesus who was dead; and he is now definitely alive. But this is a new and mysterious kind of life he lives. The scripture writers do not say Jesus came back to life in the way one goes to sleep and then wakes up again. He passed through death to a new, a better, a glorified life, and those who saw him knew it.

And thirdly, by appearing to his disciples Jesus revealed that in this new and mysterious life he no longer comes and goes; he is simply present. The evangelists' style of writing about Jesus during his earthly life is full of the details of Jesus coming to a place and then departing. We are often told how he comes and goes—he walked; he got into a boat and crossed to the other side; he entered the synagogue on the sabbath with his disciples. But their accounts of his presence after his resurrection have none of that. "Morning came and Jesus stood on the shore"; "Mary turned around and there stood Jesus"; "The disciples were in the room behind locked doors, and Jesus stood in their midst"; "And suddenly without warning Jesus stood before them and said, 'Peace.' " The only time we are told how he comes or goes is after the walk to Emmaus; Luke says that he disappeared from their sight.

Through these appearances to his disciples Jesus revealed that he is alive in a new and mysterious way in which he never again comes or goes; he's simply present. And this is the revelation that has enabled his disciples down through the centuries to proclaim that "Jesus is Lord!" Jesus had chosen a group early in his public ministry. They were to be with him—to be his disciples. They were to be sent—he would make them apostles. And when they were sent, they were to preach (kerygma)—they were to proclaim what they had witnessed by being with him.

Because he is alive in a new and mysterious way, and

because he no longer comes and goes but is simply present, it is possible for his apostles to carry out his final instructions to them: "Go, therefore, make disciples of all nations. . . . And know, I am with you always, until the end of the world" (Mt 28:19-20). A disciple is one who is *with him*. All nations can now be made disciples, because he is alive in a new and mysterious way in which he no longer comes and goes; he's just present. We can be with him, because he is forever with us.

The paschal mystery with its three movements—Jesus becoming what all people are, his acceptance of death, and his being raised to newness of life—is his personal experience. It is also the mystery of Christ which each Christian must live out in order to be his follower. It is the central mystery of Jesus' life and the central mystery of every Christian's life. Paul introduces the hymn in his letter to the Philippians by saying: "Your attitude must be that of Christ. Though he was in the form of God . . ." (Phil 2:5-6). We must try to have in ourselves that mind which was in Christ Jesus.

For each Christian the paschal mystery is a constant cyclic movement, not a once-in-a-lifetime experience. Again and again we are invited to become what all people are, to accept even death, and to come by means of that death to a newness of life.

The first and simplest expression of this mystery as Jesus lived it was the proclamation: "JESUS CHRIST IS LORD!" The New Testament authors gradually unfolded and spelled out that simple proclamation in more elaborate detail. St. John, after having almost 60 years to ponder the mystery, wrote in the Book of Revelation:

> After this I had another vision: above me there was an open door to heaven, and I heard the trumpetlike voice which had spoken to me before. It said, "Come up here and I will show you what must take place in the time to come."

> In the right hand of the One who sat on the throne I saw

a scroll. It had writing on both sides and was sealed with seven seals. Then I saw a mighty angel who proclaimed in a loud voice: "Who is worthy to open the scroll and break its seals?" But no one in heaven or on earth or under the earth could be found to open the scroll or examine its contents. I wept bitterly because no one could be found worthy to open or examine the scroll.

One of the elders said to me: "Do not weep. The Lion of the Tribe of Judah, the Root of David, has won the right by his victory to open the scroll with the seven seals."

Then, between the throne with the four living creatures and the elders, I saw a Lamb standing, a Lamb that had been slain. . . . The Lamb came and received the scroll from the right hand of the One who sat on the throne. When he had taken the scroll, the four living creatures and the twenty-four elders fell down before the Lamb. . . . This is the new hymn they sang:

"Worthy are you to receive the scroll
  and break open its seals,
  for you were slain.
With your blood you purchased for God
  men of every race and tongue,
  of every people and nation.
You made of them a kingdom
  and priests to serve our God,
  and they shall reign on the earth" (Rv 4:1;5:1-10).

John had been exiled to the island of Patmos because the Christians were living through a time of great persecution. It was a time when the believers in Jesus were liable to get discouraged. So John pondered the events his Christian community was experiencing, and he did so in the light of what he believed about the paschal mystery. In his vision he was told to "come up here and I will show you what must happen hereafter." And then he saw in the hand of God a scroll so perfectly sealed that no one could see what was inside of it. The scroll contained all the events "which must happen hereafter," all the events of human history. And there was no one who could be present to all those events, who could break the seals, except the Lamb who was standing— *alive!* — but who had been dead. This risen Lord is present to every event of human history and has dominion over them because of his victory. Even those events which escape the dominion of the Christian community—those events which go contrary to what the believers know to be right—do not escape his dominion. He can use even those to bring to completion the work he has begun.

Paul shared the same faith, and in chapter four of his letter to the Philippians, he expressed the effect that faith had on him and which it could have on all believers. He wrote: "Rejoice in the Lord always! I say it again: Rejoice! Everyone should see how unselfish you are; the Lord is near" (Phil 4:4-5). The word "unselfish" is translated in many different ways. Basically it means the state of mind and spirit which the Stoics sought—tranquility which is brought about by having no selfish concerns. There is reason to rejoice, Paul says. And the reason is not that everything is pleasant or is going the way believers know is right; the reason is that the Lord is very near, he is present, he has dominion over even those events which seem so troublesome. Through those events the Lord can accomplish his purpose.

Therefore, Christians in all of their endeavors can lay aside fear and anxious care and make it the primary business of life to have within themselves the mind that was in Christ Jesus. The Christian can become what all people are, can accept even death, and can be raised to a newness of life.

A commitment to a celibate life "for the sake of the kingdom" is one of the Christian undertakings to which some people are called. The three movements of the paschal mystery provide, I believe, the model for living out that commitment, as they provide the model for all Christian life.

And yet, in my opinion, much of the difficulty experienced by people who have made a commitment to celibacy or to married life or to the single life is that they refuse to become what all people are, they avoid and flee from death, and they refuse to be raised to the newness of life which can be theirs if they will pursue their calling in life. In the remaining chapters of this section I want to look primarily at the paschal mystery as the model for living out the call to a celibate life, although much of what I say can apply to other lasting lifestyles.

Chapter Seven

Becoming What All People Are

"I fail to understand how God could give you a penis which is horny 360 days a year and still give you the idea you are called to a celibate life," he said in response to my question about what other things preoccupied him. "And it's not just a matter of being horny in that physical sense, but also in terms of intimacy and relationship, acceptance and the need for affection."

The questioner was a 25-year-old religious brother who knows that in a year or so he will be thinking seriously about making final profession in a celibate religious community. Our conversation took place on Friday, I believe.

On Sunday I was visiting a priest with a life commitment to religious life. He had been wrestling with the same sort of question for the previous six or eight months—ever since he had fallen in love with a very wonderful woman—and he was arriving at some answers to his question.

"I learned something from Barney Miller a couple of weeks ago," he said, "and I'd like to share it with you." He described the episode on the weekly television series. One of the policemen in Barney Miller's precinct had shot and killed a man in the line of duty. And he was disconsolate. As always, most of the episode took place in the office in precinct headquarters, and it centered around this man's dealing with his dismay that he had killed someone. Other members of the force tried in a variety of ways to help the officer get over his depression. Some passed it off with attempts at humor in an effort to cheer him up. Others philosophized about it. Some in a more hard-nosed fashion just urged him to get on with life. No one was able to help.

My friend narrated the closing scene in the episode. Barney was leaving the office at the end of the day. The officer who had shot the man was still sitting at his desk. As Barney was about to leave, he turned to the policeman and said, "Did you know that the largest mammal in the world is the sperm whale?"

"No," the officer responded, looking a little puzzled.

"Do you know how large its throat is?"

"No."

Lifting his arm and holding his thumb and index finger about two inches apart, he said, "About this big."

"Oh."

"And do you know why that is?"

"No."

"Because that's the way it is, and there's nothing you can do about it!"

On Monday I shared the Barney Miller story with the brother with whom I had had the Friday conversation. In his question about being "horny" there is an assumption that things should be otherwise, or that he should be able to understand why things are the way they are, or that he should be able to do something about it. In fact that's just the way it is and there's nothing he can do about it.

I knew even then that if I ever did write a book about the celibate life, I'd try to take that brother's honest question very seriously, because I'm sure he's not the only celibate person whose question veils some assumptions about celibate life. I lived most of my life with those same assumptions. If it weren't for the grace of having a good number of healthy celibate people share their own questions and experiences with me these past dozen years, I'm pretty sure I'd still have the same assumptions. After these years of listening to others, I sometimes feel as if I am a broker of other people's experiences. Having heard their stories and having had the chance to compare their experiences with my own, I now conclude that the only reasonable answer to some of the questions is: "Because that's the way it is and there's nothing you can do about it."

Often the questions center on people's experience of simply having a body and being sexual. These are not at all connected with the fact that the person has made or is thinking of making a commitment to celibate life; they are questions born, for the most part, out of the normal human curiosity about one's own and other people's sexuality.

There is a practice among most adolescents that has become almost an accepted custom and ritual. People who are discovering the physical, emotional, personal and relational aspects of their awakening and growing sexuality almost always speak about it with their peers. They are driven to do so by a very normal sexual curiosity. But practically no one enters those conversations with any willingness to reveal that he or she is seeking information and perspective. They all act as if they are experienced and knowledgeable as they share their real or imagined "wisdom."

In growing up I was not, of course, in on all the "girl talk" about awakening sexuality, so I don't know about that. But the "boy talk" was always done with the minimum of words and the maximum of knowing glances. We shared our considerable ignorance with each other and returned to our private corners of the world to try to make sense out of what we had found out about ourselves and our friends. Each one of us, I'm sure, felt that he was the only one who really didn't know. It seemed never to occur to us that maybe the others had lied too!

I first discovered that I could use my penis for something other than going to the bathroom while I was quite young. It was a fascinating experience. I couldn't imagine why I was responding the way I was to certain stimuli, or why I suddenly had such curiosity about my own and other people's bodies. But as the other kids in the neighborhood—somewhat older than I was—introduced me to strip poker, and as we played spin the bottle on front sidewalks, I pretended that I knew all about sex and acted as if I were perfectly comfortable with my body.

Gradually I got to be familiar with my own sexual responsiveness. Our group of guys swapped stories—again, mostly lies and false impressions—about our new experience of being a man. But just knowing how I responded didn't help me know whether or not that was the way I "should" respond. And I never knew if the way I experienced being me was anything like the way other guys experienced being them. And so I never knew if I was normal or not. Some in our group were probably "turned on" by guys, but of course peer pressure kept them from ever exploring their experience. Over the years I have learned that at least I was normal in how I went about seeking to answer my questions. None of us simply asked for information from someone who could provide us with answers. We sought information while pretending we were not in need of it.

I found that in late adolescence and early adulthood the same basic pattern remains, even with the passing of generations. I remember my own embarrassment when I introduced a course on sexuality into the novitiate program. I felt sure that those novices of a new generation were much more informed than I had been at their age—maybe even more informed than I was at age 32. But I was determined not to presume anything. Experience had taught me at least that much. I had learned, for example, because I knew a man who as a novice had spoken with his spiritual director about his problem of masturbation. Two years later he confided to me that he had just discovered how to masturbate! Neither his spiritual director nor I will ever know what it was he struggled with during novitiate!

So we introduced "Clark's Fantastic Sex Course" into the novitiate curriculum. And despite my fear that I might be embarrassed by teaching things which were "old hat," I was determined to presume nothing. I even got used to the idea that they would all be sitting there *looking* like everything they were hearing was "old hat." But each year I found that I had presumed a lot. Even when novices started coming to novitiate after two, three or four years of college, and after paring my sex course down to more and more basic information, I found I still sometimes presumed that the guys had more correct information than they actually did.

I have now discovered that the confident exchange of ignorance is not only an adolescent phenomenon. People my age are not much better at sharing with one another their wonders and doubts and their experience of being sexual. On these they remain silent. Like adolescents, I suspect that adults continue the bravado of false impressions, the all-knowingness of misinformation.

By middle age we all have become very familiar with our own idiosyncratic sexual responsiveness. If we can bring ourselves to share our questions and doubts with a caring friend, we may find that we become more comfortable with ourselves. I have found that it is entirely possible for me to listen to others explore their experience and become more comfortable about themselves, even in an area where I myself am still uncomfortable. The increase of comfort and understanding comes, I suspect, from our mutual sharing of the experience, rather than from any information I have to offer.

And so, the assumptions underlying many of our questions are allowed to continue. We still say: "It shouldn't be this way. We should be able to understand why it is the way it is. We should be able to do something about it." All false assumptions!

The 25-year-old religious brother with his preoccupations about his own experience of having a body and of being sexually responsive is simply experiencing being what all people are. To be sure, the degree of comfort varies not only from one individual to another but for the same individual from one period of his or her life to another. We can almost always surprise ourselves. I am not totally comfortable with my sexuality, and I don't expect to be until shortly after they have carried me in my coffin into church. Some considerable degree of comfort is normal for mature people, but our physical responsiveness to varying stimuli, our fantasies, even our impulses and actions, will predictably startle us from time to time. To be comfortable with one's sexuality does not mean that the mystery has gone from it forever.

I think that there must be a lot of younger people in seminaries and houses of men and women religious like that 25-year-old religious brother, people asking how it is possible for God to make them the way they are and still give them the idea that they are called to a celibate life. The demeanor and discussions of the older, more established members of the seminaries and religious communities offer little evidence to suggest that they have any experience of being sexual creatures. And so the younger people understandably wonder about their fitness for the priesthood or religious life. And if they leave the seminary or religious life, they are convinced they left "because of celibacy," when in fact they may have left because they had no help in becoming what all people are.

It is not only on the level of bodily and physical sexual responsiveness that there is something to be learned by trying to have in ourselves that mind which was in Christ Jesus:

> Though he was in the form of God,
>   he did not deem equality with God
>   something to be grasped at.
> Rather, he emptied himself
>   and took the form of a slave,
>   being born in the likeness of men.

> He was known to be of human estate, . . . (Phil 2:6-8).

We can learn something for ourselves on the level of our relational, affectional and personal intimacy needs, too.

But here too there are some obstacles. Our church, our society and most individuals in both of these groups tend to look upon the celibate life and those who embrace it as something superior to the rest of society's and the church's institutions and individuals.

Our church, consciously and deliberately at times, and at other times in the manner of an unconscious prejudice, tends to regard celibacy as a superior call and those who respond to it as somehow superior to those who respond to different calls.

Many people tend to regard any attempt at a lifelong celibate commitment as foolhardy—something beyond the realm of the average human being—and they are so suspicious of the claim that they usually will not believe it. If someone who claims to have made and lived such a commitment is credible enough that people in our society can believe it, that person is looked upon often as somehow superhuman.

What is true of our church and our society generally is echoed in the attitudes of individuals in the church and society and by groups and institutions within the church and society. I find that married spirituality, for instance, is taken generally as an adjunct to the life of married couples, an adjunct derived from celibate spirituality and directed by celibates. I don't mean simply that married and single people look to celibates to gain from their perspective; I am referring to what seems to me to be an assumption that celibate spirituality is the model of all spirituality, and married or single spirituality is necessarily second-best and really not so spiritual. I'm suggesting that people in our church and society at large bombard the celibate person with an assumption that he or she is beyond or above the realm of normal human beings. It shows up in the sometimes stated, sometimes assumed attitude that a celibate commitment is more difficult, more sublime, more precarious than other life commitments.

A difficulty which falls to celibates because of the assumption that they are superior is the danger that they will be led to deny the humanity they have in common with other people. And if the denial is made, celibate men and women will be surprised when they find within themselves the same "stuff" which all people find within themselves. Their surprise will lead them to repress their humanity when they do begin to discover it, or to think that they were never called to a celibate life because they come to know, at last, that they are what all people are.

The assumption that celibate people are a cut above ordinary human beings is instilled in people while they are still very young. I can remember talking to a young man in high school and speaking with him again when he was in college. Religious life appealed to him because of the religious men he had come to know while growing up. And I thought he was the kind of man I would most want to see consider religious life. But because he knew of his own physical and emotional experience of being sexual, he was unable to seriously consider the possibility of a celibate lifestyle. He presumed that since he knew he was "horny" often and had fallen in love with several girls during high school and college, the priesthood or religious life could not be for him. The assumption: People called to a celibate life are "above all that."

I am one of the millions of people who bought and read the novel *The Thornbirds.* In the book there is a central character whose name is Ralph. When we first meet him he is a priest in a little town in Australia. He becomes a bishop, an archbishop and a cardinal. He is a marvelous man in so many ways, and I liked him from the start. But I always cringed, as I read the book, when Ralph would tell himself that he was before everything else a priest; only after that was he a man. He eventually proved that that wasn't so; he has a son, who he doesn't even know exists. The woman who bore his son never told him, and because she had a husband, the son's identity could be successfully concealed, even from the son.

The young man eventually decides to study for the priesthood, and he is sent to Rome to study—to Rome where his father is a ranking member of the Papal Curia. Somehow or other the seminarian comes to have an interview with the cardinal, his father, as part of his examination for candidacy for orders. The cardinal asks the lad if he knows what he is getting into by taking on the responsibility of a celibate life. The lad says he does. The cardinal, although he does not know that he is speaking with his own son, sees in the boy a lot of himself, and drawing on what he knows of himself, he questions the 19-year-old about human weakness. The boy responds, "But your Eminence, I'm a man first, and only then a priest." Now, in the wisdom of his increased age, the cardinal recognizes that with this humble realization the boy is better equipped to vow celibacy than the cardinal had been when he denied or belittled his humanity. And everything inside of me said, "The woman who wrote this book really does understand that celibate people are made of the same stuff everyone else is."

Another danger I see in the assumption that a celibate is superior to other people is this: Celibate people will neglect and perhaps even reject as unnecessary or unworthy of them all those normal human gestures of affection and appreciation which come to them. They will brush off expressions of gratitude and appreciation. They will ignore them and pretend even to themselves that they are unaffected by such praise or applause, and that they should be "above all that."

I suspect this second danger plays on the individual celibate man or woman in some subtle but devastating ways. It is the equivalent of starving one's self of the nourishment required for human life. If a celibate ignores or denies the kind of human esteem which meets our normal intimacy needs in ordinary ways, is it surprising that our human needs heighten to the point that we eventually begin to steal from sources not legitimate for us the kind of affection we crave? Eventually we may even "smash the bakery window" in search of a supposedly unlimited supply of what we have lived without for so long.

At the point of starvation, the danger I mentioned first—the failure to recognize that celibate people are what all people are—comes back into play. Because of the feeling of starving to death emotionally, we suspect we weren't called to a celibate commitment in the first place, and so "stealing" or "breaking into the bakery" is somehow permissible. And if it is permissible, those who will not permit it to us are obviously unfeeling and lack understanding. How else could they continue to require of us faithfulness to the commitment we made without knowing really who we were?

At the point of emotional starvation we readily admit that we *are* what all people are, and that we need affection like everyone else. But we will perhaps perpetuate the assumption that celibate people—people *truly* called to that lifestyle—are in some way superior to the rest of us. The dynamic of superiority is subtle, but I suspect it is operative on almost all levels of church and society. And I suspect it is operating to everyone's disadvantage.

I doubt if decrees or assertions from church and society can possibly counteract this prevailing assumption. It is only people with celibate commitments who can interject a contradicting voice. And even these celibate men and women cannot speak constructively to their world with mere words of protestation. Nor can they challenge the assertion of their superiority by deliberately "acting shamelessly" or in "getting down there with the rest of the folks." I think celibate people have sometimes hurt themselves by challenging the assumption of their own superiority through their *deliberate efforts* to prove by their actions that they are just like everyone else.

If a corrective statement is to be made, it can be made only by the living witness to this truth, that celibate men and women are human beings. It is only by force of their own experience of being who they are, and not by trying to *prove* something, that the assumption of their superiority can be significantly and constructively altered. Jesus didn't set out to prove something about being what all people are. He simply lived that way. And in so doing it is true that he offended some who thought no one ought to be so clearly known to be of human estate.

If as celibate men and women we can recognize that we are indeed what all people are and accept *without demanding* the affective and intimate expressions which come to us from others, we will be making a contribution toward correcting the prevailing assumptions. If we allow people to know that our human needs have been met by the appreciation, affirmation and affection they have freely offered, then we are acknowledging our needs. We are saying that we are what all people are. But if we let our needs be known by *demanding* that they be met, we will frighten off those who will wonder if they have the resources to provide us with what we need. Perhaps worse yet, if we insist on remaining hard-nosed, dedicated people who show no signs of needing or appreciating what others give us, we will be starving ourselves, and we will be telling others that celibate people are "above all that."

It is one thing to tell someone we need intimacy and affection. It is quite another thing to acknowledge graciously that someone's sharing of his or her life, expression of gratitude or offer of affection is recognized, accepted and appreciated. It is one thing to *demand* that someone listen to me because "I have needs too"; it is quite another thing to *thank* someone sincerely for having listened.

I, a celibate person, am what all people are. If I mistakenly think that I have some superhuman ability to continually meet other people's needs, I delude myself. My commitment to a celibate life does not even mean I should have this ability to equal God in giving to others without the need to receive from them. If I recognize my inability to always provide a listening ear, sympathetic word, affectionate reassurance, appreciative glance, supportive stance, graceful gesture, without receiving the same from others, I have discovered what it takes to live in this human estate. In recognizing my capacity to give to others and my need to receive from them, I have discovered that others have the capacity to meet my needs. I make this acknowledgement by graciously receiving what is freely offered.

At times I will have to live without having my needs met. At times I will be invited to enter fully and vulnerably into life's moments of loneliness because I have a commitment to stand ready to do so. At times what I know I need is simply not going to be available from other human beings. And at those times I can rediscover the radical all-sufficiency of God. By their commitment to stand ready to enter fully and vulnerably into life's moments of intimacy, others have secured for themselves at least the possibility of a lasting source of reciprocal human love. I have not chosen that life, but my commitment to celibacy does not mean that I am called to walk blithely through life, passing up those things which are freely offered and which do in fact feel good because they meet my needs.

I think the gracious flow of affection, appreciation, gratitude and affirmation is what is expected of people who do not have a celibate commitment. The give-and-take of such intimate relationships is presumed. I believe that most people recognize that such vulnerable and transparent presence of people to one another can lead to ongoing commitments to one another. And such relating can lead to romantic intimacy and eventually to mutual emotional dependence and to making genital-sexual commitments. But I fear that some think that such a development is not only *normal*, but that it is also *inevitable*.

I have a friend who has often said that we used to watch the boy-meets-girl scene in a movie and wonder *if* they would go to bed together; nowadays we wonder only *when* they will go to bed together. There seems to have been a shift in our expectations about how intimate relationships develop.

People used to recognize that intimacy *could* develop into romance, which in turn could lead one to make genital-sexual commitments to another. Now such development seems inevitable. And I think this sense of inevitability contributes to making celibate people shy away from normal intimate relationships in fear that they must necessarily lead to romantic intimacy. Maybe it would be better, some tell themselves, to ignore or deny the normal intimacy needs and to avoid altogether the normal ways they can be met, rather than get into a situation which will inevitably lead to romantic pursuits.

I recognize that one of the normal outcomes of becoming increasingly transparent and vulnerable to another is to become romantically involved and eventually to make sexual and genital commitments. But I resent the implication that what is normal is also inevitable.

All commitments evolve. This is true of the commitment to a lifelong style of living, be it married, single or celibate. But, to think that because there is a normal evolutionary process to every commitment means that there is a path leading inevitably to each commitment bothers me.

I suspect that *romantic* intimacy will lead to marriage with a force that seems to approximate inevitability. But romantic intimacy is already sexual in a way that invites emotional and genital commitments. But all intimacy is not romantic.

Many religious and priests with a celibate commitment have discovered their capacity for intimacy and their need for it, but some of them have refused to acknowledge that they have that need and capacity fearing that they will inevitably be led into romantic intimacy. Then, if they finally do acknowledge that the capacity and the need are there, they may begin to allow a commitment to *romantic* intimacy to evolve, believing that the normal process they are experiencing is also inevitable.

People have forgotten that they have some control over

what they will do with their needs and capacities regarding intimacy. They cannot control the fact that they have them, but they can control the expression of them. My own celibate commitment evolved over the course of many years. Having now made the deliberate choice and commitment to what evolved, I believe that part of it is to keep contrary commitments from evolving. To discover continually that I am what all people are does not mean that I must do what most people do. To discover continually that I am sexual and that I have a capacity for romantic love does not mean that I will inevitably pursue romantic intimate relationships. Having come to know that I am what all people are, I need to have in myself again the mind that was in Christ Jesus, who

> Though he was in the form of God,
> . . . did not deem equality with God
> something to be grasped at.
> Rather, he emptied himself
> and took the form of a slave,
> being born in the likeness of men.

> He was known to be of human estate, . . . (Phil 2:6-8).

And being what all people are, he was humbler still, *even to accepting death.*

In the next chapter we will reflect more fully on the meaning the second movement of the paschal mystery has for those committed to a celibate life. For now it is enough to recall that intimacy is not inevitably romantic and romantic intimacy need not inevitably be pursued. There is the possibility of mortification and the invitation to accept even death. But if the need for intimacy inevitably led to romantic intimacy, and if romantic intimacy inevitably led to emotional dependence and genital commitments, then it would be true that only someone who is more than human (or less than human) could make a commitment to celibate life.

To be committed to a celibate life does not mean that one is superior to other human beings. To recognize that one is put together in just the same way that all people are does not mean that one is not called to a life of celibacy. Celibate people are what all people are, and that's just the way it is and there's nothing you can do about it!

Thank you, Barney Miller!

Chapter Eight

Accepting Even Death

Death is difficult to do much clear thinking about because of all the feelings we have about it. We spend most of our life avoiding the subject, and if we do think about it, it is most likely to be from the perspective of familiar occupations and interests.

Death is much like loneliness. It's not much fun to think about. If the experience of death impinges on us to the point that we are forced to reflect on it, our first reaction is often to think of how it interrupts and puts an end to so much of what was going on—not just for the individual who has died, but for the survivors as well.

I remember attending the funeral of a high-school senior who died as the result of a freak sports injury. I did not know the boy, but I attended his funeral with a good friend who was also very close to the boy's family. The football jersey, the crossed water skis, the letter jacket embossed with the year of graduation—the presence of all these items in the church recalled the boy's life and spoke startlingly of the interruption of his habits, goals and plans.

The reaction of most people isn't much different when death calls a 35-year-old priest and religious. I stood in the sanctuary of a seminary chapel as the celebrant of a funeral Mass for Jim, a brother Capuchin younger than I. All of us assembled recalled his life and tried to understand why a perfectly healthy man's heart had just stopped and why God could ask this of Jim or his family or the seminary where he was slated to be rector. We could not avoid thinking about death on such an occasion, so we tried to make sense out of it. But we were hampered by our sense that it couldn't possibly be right because it caused so much suffering and was so unexpected.

A few years ago our province buried an 87-year-old religious brother who had retained much of his physical strength until shortly before his death, although hardening of the arteries had reduced his completely lucid moments to rare occurrences. He had lived a full life of religious dedication to the ordinary tasks of life, but his death was still not a pleasant thing to have to deal with.

When we are forced to think about death because someone we knew and loved has died, we tend to think in religious terms. We are grateful for our faith to fall back on because it gives us a way of dealing with what is painful but inevitable.

As I sit here on a sunny afternoon, presumably in good health and not having to deal with the death of someone close to me, I can think about death and not have to think of it only from the perspective of how it affects me. But I don't expect that my philosophizing will do much good the next time I have a chest pain and wonder if it is the apples I ate or the first sign of an impending coronary.

This afternoon, death can and does look perfectly normal and predictable. It certainly represents the *limitation of life*—the limitation known from our earliest years, but recognized in its full force only when it claims a boy and we look at the football jersey and water skis; or when we recount the deeds of 87 years of life for Brother George.

Death represents the limitation of something good. It's a limitation we know is there, but which doesn't affect us personally until we have to say yes to that limitation in some way that means our own life has to change a bit or a lot. And yet, despite this limitation, death frees us from the other limitations we have faced all during life.

The New Testament writers expressed the view that

death is not only a limitation of human life, but also that through death Jesus shed the limitations of human life. They also tell us that Jesus responded to the prospect of his death in the same way we do. He asked his Father if it couldn't be avoided altogether. When he saw he could not avoid it, he faced it with his beliefs about its correctness although it seems that it wasn't his own idea—"Your will, not mine be done." But previous to the moment of facing its closeness, Jesus had spoken of it and thought of it as his glorification, as the shedding of his human limitations.

Death did not destroy Jesus' human life. It transformed it. All human beings have to accept that the inevitable limitation of death does not in fact destroy their lives. But we couldn't know this if it weren't for Jesus.

He gives this experience of the limitedness of human life the assurance that it is also the shedding of the limitations of human life. And it is this paschal experience of Jesus that all Christians are urged to take part in if they want in themselves the mind which was also in Christ Jesus, who ". . . accepted even death." The celibate man or woman, as well as any other Christian, was "baptized unto his death."

Accepting even death is mortification, and it is a necessary limitation on human life. By *accepting even death*, accepting this limitation, we also shed the limitations of human life without ceasing to be human. At least in a symbolic way, we accept even death when we acknowledge or accept limitation in our lives. Let me explain.

When I began teaching "Clark's Fantastic Sex Course" (the title was devised mainly to assure me that it was worthwhile), I bought Herder and Herder's *Sex Book*. Although it purported to be an encyclopedia of sexual information, it editorialized an amorality I find objectionable. However, the definition of asceticism which I found there is still one of the best I have found anywhere:

> Asceticism: Renunciation of pleasure in favor of some special goal. In a sense, we are all ascetics. Every life offers more

possibilities than can be explored. Everyone has to restrict himself and constantly has to give up something in order to get something else. There is an inescapable, permanent, and occasionally frustrating necessity to make selections. In short, our lives are made up of innumerable individual choices according to some basic set of priorities.

This definition bears witness to the fact that we crave more than we can have. No matter what we crave, once we have experienced it, the moment passes. We crave for it to be permanent, but it never is. A total sense of well-being, a moment of great intimacy, profound thankfulness or complete joy, will not be permanent. We either accept this limitation or we will become resentful and cynical, and begin to deny the beauty and value of those human experiences simply because they didn't last. By accepting this limitation we are *accepting even death*, and being freed from a limitation of life. If we will not accept the death which is a natural part of human life, we will not engage ourselves any longer in human life.

Recently I enjoyed two very satisfying days of intimate conversations with a friend. I had been alone in a primitive cabin in the woods; I was working on this manuscript. After six days of solitude, a friend joined me for the weekend. Being alone had been good for me, and I think our being together was good for both of us.

On Tuesday morning he got into his car and left. That night I left the cabin where I had pumped and carried water, cooked my own meals, started my own fire and worked in solitude. But just before I left, I sat and reflected on the week. Solitude and intimacy! Two profound human experiences. And now both were ending. But neither, I knew, was less real because it was not permanent. Both disposed me for other similar moments, other moments of solitude with different things to learn, other moments of intimacy with different people whom I would allow to know me.

Although I hated to see those moments end, I knew it was normal and necessary. But I also knew I craved more of both solitude and friendship than those moments had provided.

I experience this same sort of necessity to accept even death in order to choose life in a hobby I have. Most of my work is not very tangible—at least in its results. I spend most days and a good share of my evenings speaking with people and doing personnel planning for our province. At the end of a day, I never really know what, if anything, I have accomplished. I often envy those who work with their hands. They can see what they've done.

My hobby is making sandals. I don't attempt to make sandals for the friars who ask me for a pair unless at the time they ask I am in need of some "therapy." If I decide to spend a couple hours a day for two or three days custom making a pair of sandals for someone, when I finish I am faced with that "inescapable, permanent and occasionally frustrating" experience of accepting even death in order to choose life. The sandals are finished; I can see what I've accomplished. I rejoice in my workmanship. But I experience some small death as I realize it is useless for me just to see them, that I must give them to the person they were made for.

The only alternatives I see to accepting even death are to become cynical about life because its great moments don't last, or to set out on a pursuit of self-fulfillment by doing all it takes in order to attain all that I crave. Cynicism doesn't appeal to me; and I've yet to meet a person always in hot pursuit of self-fulfillment who shows any real signs of being happy.

So, on a sunny afternoon filled with the leisure time to philosophize, accepting even death seems like a normal part of life. It does not threaten. However I'm sure my feelings about dealing with the kind of death which life demands won't change much because of my having spent the afternoon with my thoughts about it. Hopefully my thinking will influence how I will deal with life's death-moments even though with my feelings I still try to avoid them.

I believe it is a realistic hope. And maybe if as celibates we think about the necessity of accepting even death before we are faced with the experience, then we too, for all our feelings, could be a little more able to pursue something other than self-fulfillment.

In anyone's life, seeking self-fulfillment is the opposite of accepting even death. And it has some special consequences for the celibate since part of the celibate's social witness is to say clearly that self-fulfillment is not the ultimate meaning of life.

I once heard a married woman say that Christian married couples need Christian celibates within the believing community in order to show the world what distinguishes Christian marriages from others.

Christian marriage is a sacrament because it is a sign of something real but invisible, namely, Christ's selfless love for his church. A celibate commitment is not a sacrament because it points to what is visible in Christian marriage, but which is easily missed or misunderstood, namely, that self-fulfillment is not the ultimate meaning of life.

The "bottom line" for Christians who take each other for life no matter what, must be a selfless love which is a visible expression of Christ's selfless love in taking his church to himself. Celibates within the same believing community highlight this dimension of Christian marriage by living in a way that recognizes that self-fulfillment is not the ultimate meaning of life.

Self-fulfillment can be sought in many ways, and therefore the invitation to accept even death is a rather constant one for everybody. The temptation of celibates to seek self-fulfillment can be recognized in at least two areas where they have distinguished themselves from other believing Christians—dealing with physical and emotional needs, and personal intimate relationships. The need to accept even death is not greater for celibates in these areas, but the particular way of doing so is different from that of married couples.

Depending on their sexual orientation and on many factors in their childhood, celibate people find themselvs to be sexually responsive to many kinds of stimuli.

Once we know ourselves to be sexually responsive there is almost always the temptation to *seek* sexual response. We can find ourselves being sexually responsive and know that we do not have to do anything about it. Contrary to popular opinion, we do not have to act out sexual urges, and we do not have to make them go away.

I was helped to arrive at the conclusion that we can be sexually responsive and not have to do anything about it by a good friend who was my spiritual director for years. I could predict that some things would evoke a physical and emotional sexual response in me. At other times I was surprised to find myself responding that way. But gradually I came to know that that's just the way I am. Years later I shared with a younger friend what I had come to accept as true of me. He had lived for years with the assumption that when he found himself "horny" he was in for a struggle which would eventually end in his masturbating. So, he was beginning to conclude that he might as well do it now, get it over with and save himself a lot of struggle! I suggested to him that his assumptions about the inevitability of acting on his sexual desires were not well-founded and that he might try changing his assumptions. I asked him to consult with his spiritual director about the matter and to check out my "theory." Later he said, "You're right." Encouraged, I told others, and they too said it was true of their own experience.

It's one thing to be sexually responsive; it's another thing altogether to seek sexual response. The first is simply being what all people are. The second is, for the celibate man or woman, refusing to accept even death. How does one recognize the difference between being sexually responsive and seeking sexual response? By a relaxed honesty with one's self.

For some celibate people accepting the fact that they are sexually responsive is a problem; they have a difficult time entering into the first movement of the paschal mystery. If they eventually do accept that they are indeed what all people are they sometimes feel that they must give vent to their newly discovered sexual responsiveness and act out those things they have just discovered about themselves. Now the second movement of the paschal mystery is posing a difficulty and offering a challenge. Other celibates never had any difficulty accepting that they were what all people are, but they fear they will lose or deny their humanity if they do not act out their sexuality in romantic and genital ways. On the physical and emotional level, and on the level of personal intimate relationships, the invitation is there to accept even death—the shedding of human limitations—without ceasing to be human. Human sexuality and its romantic and genital expression are not human limitations; for celibates, however, pursuing romantic intimacy and indulging in genital-sexual expression is a human limitation of sin and selfishness, because it is contrary to their commitment.

The celibate man or woman is committed to accepting fully his or her humanity with all its drives and needs and capacities. He or she is also committed to a way of life which does not act out those drives, needs and capacities in pursuing romantic intimacy or genital-sexual commitments. Celibate people may at times become involved in a moment of romantic intimacy. Celibate people respond romantically like everyone else does. But because of their commitment they will not *pursue* that kind of intimacy with another. An intimate moment can be romantic if either by design or effect it invites us toward emotional dependence or toward making genital-sexual commitments. A celibate will at times find an intimate moment romantic by effect. But a commitment to celibacy means, I believe, that a celibate man or woman will not enter a moment of intimacy which is romantic by design.

There is a normal and very beautiful process of involvement in romantic intimacy. By pursuing it, two people consent to the evolution of an emotional dependence and perhaps eventually to a genital-sexual commitment to each other in marriage. A celibate commitment is incompatible with such pursuits, it seems to me. Not only are marriage and celibacy mutually exclusive ways of life but those things which lead naturally to a commitment to marriage are excluded by a celibate way of life. It is one of those normal "deaths"—a normal limitation through which celibacy is possible. Mutual bonds of emotional dependence, if they are freely chosen and personal, are beautiful human realities. But they are not part of the celibate person's life. It is a limitation on the celibate way of life which opens the celibate person to fully live his or her own chosen life.

Again, I want very much to be understood. I am not suggesting that celibate people don't have mutual emotional bonds with other people. But those bonds are not bonds of *dependence.* When celibates establish emotional bonds of intimacy and friendship, it is true that everyone is better off for having come together, but no one is worse off for parting. That cannot possibly be true of those who have committed themselves to the romantic intimacy and the genital-sexual relationship of marriage with its commitment to establish and maintain a family unit. In marriage mutual bonds of emotional dependence are essential. Not establishing such bonds is the particular form of death through which celibates attain the fullness of the life which is distinctly their own.

Conversely, a married couple that pursues the kind of relationship which excludes romantic intimacy and the establishment of mutual bonds of emotional dependence will attain the freedom and availability which are typical of a celibate lifestyle. But they will never attain the depth of life which could be theirs if they surrendered their availability to others in favor of those things which could give depth to their own kind of life. Each kind of life has its own demand to accept even death in order to attain life.

Enough of theory! Enough of philosophy! I want to put some flesh on the philosophical bones by sharing two experiences. One is a reflection on an intimate relationship I have with one of my Capuchin brothers. The other is a midnight porch-swing conversation I had with Don and Mary, friends who have shared their married life with me.

Paul was one of the deacons-to-be in the A-frame. He was ordained a deacon, and a year later a priest. I had been Paul's spiritual director nine years earlier when he was a novice. By a strange turn of events, Paul's first assignment after his ordination was to the novitiate team. By an even stranger turn of events I was unexpectedly reassigned to the novitiate team. Marty, who headed the new team and who had been my teacher right after I was ordained, had asked for both Paul and me. I went back to Saint Felix Friary in Huntington, Indiana, where I had spent my young adulthood, anticipating spending at least three years of my middle life there. But after one year I was elected vicar provincial and I had to move to Detroit.

After six weeks in Detroit, I missed Paul and Marty. One night I was thinking of Paul, and I realized I was going through something very deep inside regarding my relationship with him.

First of all, I missed him lots and realized that often. The previous year in Huntington was very important to me—better in many ways than I could have imagined, although I had thought my expectations had been too high ever to be met. And I missed the chance to sit up late and talk with Paul and to listen to him. I could share with him my own life as I could share it with very few people—probably no one but Marty. And I learned from Paul, and grew closer to him than I had been when he was a novice nine years earlier.

Secondly, and more deeply, I could feel that closeness waning, simply because the contact with him was now limited and our friendship couldn't be so easily nourished. I was getting caught up in new pursuits and new relationships with new people. Initially this embarrassed me and made me sad. I even felt a little guilty about the fact that I didn't think of him as much as I had just a month previously. But I could see how normal and even healthy that was. I knew the moments of intimacy we had shared were not less real just because they were not permanent.

And at an even deeper level, I knew I was once more experiencing the inevitable choice of letting go again. I had let go of Paul when he had left novitiate and had gone to Crown Point for college. I had made it a point during his college years and after not to intrude into his life, because I had believed he did not need me to follow him. My love and concern—even my attachment—had remained, though.

Now, sitting in Detroit, I didn't feel it was particularly for Paul's or my special good that I let go of him. It was merely the natural and inevitable consequence of celibate availability to others. Oh, I mourned the passing of the goodness and pleasure and even the pain of the times we had spent together, as I had grieved the loss of other beautiful things in my life.

But it seemed to me then, as it seems to me now, that friends drift apart when friendship isn't nourished. I knew Paul would grow and change and so would I. And the opportunity to share with each other the fascinations and frustrations of our growth would no longer be an immediately available possibility. Oh, we'd "bring each other up-to-date" when we met. And I knew I'd be glad to hear of his life when we had the chance to talk. But there was no longer the day-to-day opportunity to live through the choices and decisions together.

This time it was different from when we had parted after his novitiate. This time there was nothing so intentional about our separation. This time it was just happening.

And as I saw it happening and recognized it for what it

was, I merely noted it and smiled and cried a bit. And I became immensely more thankful to God for Paul than I had ever been.

Ah, celibacy! The pain of it is part of its beauty. Maybe even the beauty of it cannot be except in the pain of it.

I thanked God that night for the profound beauty in the ordinariness of life. There was no drama there; just the simple inevitable realities of my life. And I loved them. I thank God for making me the way I am. I thank him for feelings and for friendship. I thank him for closeness and for distance. And that night, in giving thanks for the way life was, I marvelled at how much God loves each person and at how non-coercive and non-possessive and non-manipulative he is about loving. And I thanked him for all those who had loved me in a way which prepared me to love celibately.

There is a death in loving that way—a limitation on what I crave. But there is life in accepting that death. And I don't feel any less human for accepting even death. But I do feel the pain of it and the beauty of it.

And the porch swing! One night shortly after I had returned to Saint Felix Friary some practicality of life took me to Don and Mary's house which was filled with relatives in town for a funeral the following day. Practicalities having been taken care of, I got up to leave. Don accompanied me to the door and walked me out onto the porch. "Sit down for a minute," he said. The minute turned into an hour, and eventually Mary came out to see what was keeping Don. We had been talking of what Don called their drifting away from involvement in religious pursuits. "Our priorities are all screwed up," he said. As Mary appeared on the porch, Don said, "Your turn," and gave Mary his place next to me on the porch swing; he went inside. With no prompting from Don, Mary talked about the same topic.

After Mary and I had talked for almost an hour, Don returned to the porch to "see how you two are doing." He joined us, and as our conversation continued, they told me that they looked to a celibate person for something they didn't think they could get from others. I thought of something I had recently heard in a lecture: "Most people today are not passionately devoted to any religious affiliation as they used to be; they're spiritual nomads willing to wander from one thing to another in search of whatever it is they are looking for." I think I heard Don and Mary tell me that night and early morning that they felt like spiritual nomads— spiritual, to be sure, but wandering. And they told me that they looked to me or to Tom or to Ray or to their pastor for some direction in their wandering. And they, at least, thought a celibate person could give that direction.

I have reflected on that porch-swing conversation often since we parted at around two o'clock in the morning. We talked a little about celibacy that night, because another Capuchin to whom they had been very close had just left the order to marry. And Don and Mary compared my life to their own. They told me what they expected of me because of my celibate commitment. "You don't belong to anybody like Don and I belong to each other," Mary said. "And you shouldn't. And no one can ever own you." I told her that I didn't think I had ever been owned by anybody.

The next day that phrase came back to me and I wrote it down. And I have reflected on it often. Part of being celibate means that I am owned by no one. I'm close to, involved with, yes; but I'm not anyone's property. I'm not thinking of any subjugation or domination, but of the very beautiful human longing and experience of intimacy which is so total that two people give themselves to each other for life. Somehow to say, "my priest" or "my brother" or "my sister" in respect to a celibate does not mean the same thing as to say, "my husband" or "my wife."

A celibate is a pilgrim in a generation of spiritual nomads. The only difference between a pilgrim and a nomad is that a pilgrim knows where he or she is going and a nomad just wanders. Don and Mary had said they had wandered.

And they looked to a celibate to help them know that self-fulfillment is not the ultimate meaning of life.

As I reflected on my own longing to give myself to another, I knew I had better renew continually that entry into life's moments of loneliness to find God concrete. If as a celibate, I do not come to know *experientially* that I am owned by God, something in me will remain incomplete. The very non-ownedness which I experience in relation to other human beings—and my accepting this death—is itself a meaningful element, I learned from Don and Mary, in knowing and revealing that I am owned by my God. By entering fully and vulnerably into life's moments of loneliness—which I am able to do because I am nobody's—I cultivate that sense of being owned by God which allows me to move about among my brothers and sisters as one who is theirs, not because they own me, but because I belong to *their* God, the God they meet in entering fully and vulnerably into life's moments of intimacy.

I'm enlivened and exhausted by my philosophizing and my remembering. I still doubt that my philosophizing about how death is a normal limitation on life, and a way of shedding the limitations of life, will have any effect on my feelings when next I am asked to accept the death which will give life to my celibate commitment. But my remembering of a celibate relationship with Paul and of a porch-swing conversation with Don and Mary has encouraged me. And I have just this moment realized that next month Don and Mary's oldest son will make his first vows in the Capuchin Order. I guess I am not the only one they taught about accepting even death.

♣ *Chapter Nine*

Experiencing New Life

Death is never chosen by healthy people as an end in itself. Nor did Jesus choose death for that reason. He accepted even death, death on a cross.

> Because of this,
> God highly exalted him
> and bestowed on him the name
> above every other name.

> So that at Jesus' name
> every knee must bend
> in the heavens, on the earth,
> and under the earth,
> and every tongue proclaim
> to the glory of God the Father:
> JESUS CHRIST IS LORD! (Phil 2:9-11).

All Christians are called to have in themselves the mind which was in Christ Jesus. And in accepting even death, Christians know that they come to a newness of life.

We all experience a continuing necessity to choose death in order for our chosen way of life to continue to be. I have learned from every celibate man and woman, from every dedicated single person, and from every married couple I know, that new life comes through death, not despite or instead of it.

Celibate men and women who accept the kind of dying their life requires, experience a newness of life for themselves, and a newness of life for others. New life for the individual celibate comes in ways I have already described. If I accept the death of being owned by no one, I know the newness of life of belonging to everyone because I belong to the God of these people.

Only if celibate men and women accept the death of entering fully and vulnerably into the wall of fog, will they experience being owned by God. I can't explain that any further. Those who have experienced it can't possibly miss the meaning. It is a personal, spiritual and contemplative experience of newness of life.

Only if celibate men and women accept the death of being emotionally and physically what all people are, will they experience a newness of life. They will sense an integrity which would not be theirs if they ever pursued romantic intimacy or genital involvements.

I don't feel I can say much that will make a lot of sense about newness of life. It comes through accepting even death. And those who have accepted even death know about it. Those who haven't can't possibly understand. It *is* a contemplative experience. Something in me wants to apologize for saying that, because there is a part of me which is terribly rational. I can use my rational abilities to explain the necessity of accepting even death—it's the longest chapter in this book, for gosh sake!—and I willingly do so because we are the ones who by God's grace have to accept even death. But the newness of life is beyond our rational analysis. It is God who gives that.

Part of every Christian's faith is believing that Jesus has been made Lord of every event of human history. Sometimes we think we can see how he exercises his dominion over these events. At other times we know we can't see. But whether or not we think we understand how things make sense, Jesus is Lord of every event. Celibates will often have to face death and may feel sure that the events which brought death to them have escaped Jesus' dominion.

"Why do I feel this way?" "Why must I choose death?" "Why can't things be different, Barney Miller?" celibates will ask. Every tongue must proclaim to the glory of God the Father: Jesus Christ is Lord! Many things, even most things, may escape our dominion; they have not escaped his dominion, because he has been given the name above every other name: He is Lord!

I frankly wish I could explain more fully how celibates experience new life within because of accepting the kinds of death a celibate life demands. But I can't. I want to share with you another way I have found new life in accepting the death my celibate commitment requires. But here too, I am embarrassed, because I have to lay rationality aside. I can't prove, even to myself, that what I want to say is true. But I have come to believe it.

I write almost every night in my green-book, a practice resulting from years of encouragement by one spiritual director after another, as well as friends and colleagues. I am completely honest with myself in my green-book. I write anything that trots through my mind. It provides me with a record of my ups and downs, my inspired moments and my confusions.

One night I was writing about the events of the day and I recorded what someone had said to me. He had said that after several months of sort of counseling and spiritual direction with me, he was beginning to believe that God loved him. Two days later I wrote about some letters I had received from two people, one a close friend, the other a seminarian who had made a retreat I had conducted. Both had written to say that they knew that God loved them, and that they had heard that clearly because of some contact they had had with me. They said I was a nice guy and that they liked me, but that was not what made them write. They had come to know more surely that God loved them, and somehow in their minds that was connected with me.

I pulled one letter out of the wastebasket—I had answered it already—and got the other one off my desk. And I paged back through my green-book to read what I had written in the weeks previous to my coming into contact with these two people. They had been times of immense loneliness, loneliness which I did not try to escape, but which I entered into, because I had come to know that God could be found concrete there. But until that night, despite the fact that I knew of the value for myself of entering fully and vulnerably into life's moments of loneliness, I had never felt that I could point to any fruits of that experience.

I knew that if married couples entered into life's moments of intimacy fully and vulnerably, there was the possibility of new life. I had reflected on how, for all its necessary exclusivity, married intimacy must remain open to the couple's sharing their lives with others. At least to be a full and vulnerable entry into intimacy, the couple had to be open to the possibility of sharing each of their lives with a child who could possibly be born. But I had found no similar reality for myself as a celibate man who entered fully and vulnerably into life's moments of loneliness. Now I was beginning to see!

By my full and vulnerable entry into life's moments of loneliness I experience new life in myself because I find God concrete. And finding God concrete, I become more able to have intimate, though non-romantic, experiences with other human beings which are not entered into out of my own need and which do not end in an increased intimacy only between me and the other. By my presence to others, they come to know that God loves them.

That night as I sat on my blanket before my lighted candle holding two letters in my hands, it became a little more clear to me that there was a connection between the emptiness and loneliness I had felt previous to meeting these two people and my ability to be transparent enough in my loving them that they could come to know God more fully as he really is: one who loves unconditionally.

At that point all I had was the evidence recorded in my green-book: periods of intense loneliness entered into somewhat grudgingly, but eventually fully and vulnerably. Sometimes they were followed by a realization on the part of those with whom I later shared intimate moments that they are loved by me, and by God!

I began to check others' experience for any similarity. Most people really couldn't recall what they experienced when. Many knew that they experienced loneliness and experienced others telling them that they helped them realize God's love for them. But only a few could positively make the connection between the two experiences. I kept asking people.

Two months after I first realized all this, I participated in a program for young men interested in joining our province. One of the speakers told a very moving story of a high-school senior whose life was ended by some disease. At first the boy was resentful as he lay in his hospital bed waiting for death. But the speaker told us that a couple of months later, right before the boy died, he was very peaceful and he was convinced that God loved him. The speaker had ministered to the boy all during his illness. After he finished, I asked him if he could remember his own experience during the time he was ministering to the dying boy. "An empty, desolate loneliness," he said.

I continued to be aware of my own moments of loneliness and I began to expect that as a result of my entering them, somebody with whom I shared transparently would come to know he or she was loved by God. And I continued to ask others about their experience. I am now convinced that a celibate person who will accept the death of entering fully and vulnerably into life's moments of loneliness will experience new life within because he or she comes to know God concrete. That person will also give new life to others by being the instrument through which God reveals himself to those others.

I almost decided back in 1962 not to make solemn profession. I had taken a course in marriage and family life during my final year of college, and I wasn't at all sure I wanted to give up the chance to pass my life on to another human being. Three months before I was supposed to make my final commitment to a celibate way of life, I told my spiritual director I was having second thoughts about it. "Brother," he said, "you're just suffering from a severe case of normality." He assured me that celibate people give life. Fourteen years later I knew he was right. What I have been told to be true of all men is probably equally true of all women—we all want to plant a tree, have a child and write a book.

On the basis of experience, I understand that people who in a moment of loneliness come into contact with their essential separateness, incompleteness and neediness will be able to meet and address that same separateness, incompleteness and neediness in others with an altruistic, non-possessive love. They come to know that God accepts and embraces us fully and that he alone fully meets our neediness, separateness and incompleteness.

When a person comes to know how fragile he or she is, that person can also respond to the fragileness of others. But I am not speaking only of a physical reality. I'm speaking about a spiritual, contemplative and even mystical experience. I can explain how an ovum is impregnated by a sperm and new life begins. But I can't look at Vince and Jody's daughter, Sarah, and think only of a sperm and an ovum; God is involved in all new life!

I shared with Vince the evening of Sarah's birth. He knew he had given her life. But her birth also gave him new life. And in giving birth to Sarah Jody also received new life. I don't feel that much different from Vince and Jody. There is an accepting of even death in a celibate way of life. But through that death people come to new life. They know God loves them. And I am enlivened by knowing that I have had a part in giving that life.

I wrote a letter once to a religious man who was in the midst of becoming what all people are and of accepting even death. I don't know if I even mailed it to him, because it was more my reflection on myself than anything I wanted to say to him. I wrote it in my green-book very late one night. Permit me.

> Jerry. Oh, Jerry. You again make me wonder about those things within me that you struggle with within yourself. But I've let you know me as much as I know how. I've tried to interpret my own experience in a way that my thoughts and my reflections can speak to you. And I've tried to leave you free. The last time we were together I let you know me, and you were so transparent to me that I could hear things you didn't put into words. You allowed me to do for you what you were doing for yourself: saying, "Jerry, you're a good man."
>
> And you caused me to reflect in ways deeper than I have up to now on the mystery of being what all people are. Each of us is sexual in our own way, and each of us has our own way of experiencing it. When we're in love, we experience it in its most beautiful and relational way.
>
> You have been experiencing an almost unbelievable expanding of your sense of being glad you are you. But you haven't noticed that. You were captivated—as we all are at times, Jerry—by the thought of acting out your experience of being sexual. And captivated by that prospect, everything in you that said no seemed to be an unwarranted and dehumanizing inhibition. And everything and everyone outside of you that suggested you remain faithful to your celibate commitment seemed to place unreal demands on you. "How can I be happy for Paul because he has fallen in love?" you asked me. Just as I am happy for you. When I am not captivated by the thought of acting out my sexuality in pursuing romantic intimacy, I can see what my experience of being sexual does for me as a human being.
>
> Yes, you too are invited to accept freely even death, the death of mortifying by choice your inclination to act out your sexuality in a romantic or genital way. But the new life which is already yours through this kind of death is obvious. The new life comes through the death, Jerry, not along with it. Your increased realization that you are what all people are

and your continued acceptance of the death to the thought of acting out your sexuality by pursuing romantic intimacy will enlarge you beyond what you can imagine. You can see it already in your increase of self-acceptance. And as the struggle continues you will hear from others what you do for them. You will give them life in ways you can't imagine. And you will be theirs, not because they own you, but because you belong to their God.

But the death is also real. There will be self-doubt. There will be doubt about your motivation for remaining committed to a celibate life. "Is it fear of closeness that keeps me from becoming romantically involved?" you will ask yourself over and over again. "Will I stunt or mutilate myself if I don't give rein to my inclination to act out my sexuality in a moment of romantic intimacy?" You may even seek out a trusted friend or a professional counsellor to question. And the friend won't be able to lay aside your doubts for you. And so you will struggle. And you will know how fragile you really are.

And, Jerry, people will seek you out, and you won't understand why. They will tell you what you do for them and you won't want to believe it. And you will do for them things which you thought you would never do. They will know they are loved—not only by you because you are so loving, but by God because they discover themselves at last lovable. They will thank you, and you'll be pleased. You'll know that you didn't draw on what was your supposed strength to help them. You drew on the richness of your own weakness in your struggle not to cling to equality with God, but to become what all people are. You drew on the richness of your struggle to accept even death.

You will do and say and share what you never dreamed you had within you to do or say or share. And new life will be not only within you, but around you. And you will reflect on it all some night, and fall in a crumpled heap on the ground and you will thank your God. And your whole being—your strengths *and* your weakness—will proclaim the greatness of the Lord. And you will know with certainty that all generations will declare that you have been blessed.

And someday you may hear a younger man's invitation

to do for him what he most wants done, whether it is to listen to him or to accept him. And you will hear, not because he asks in words which make sense to your mind, but because you will know how fragile he sometimes feels, because you've felt that way yourself.

The celibate person's entry into the three movements of the paschal mystery is summed up for me in three songs. They are older songs now, but they still move me every time I hear them.

The first is Roberta Flack's rendition of "The First Time Ever I Saw Your Face." In this song the part of me which is drawn to romantic intimacy finds expression. It captures so well the progression of romantic love as I imagine it to be that I have been captivated by the song. It has come to represent for me, my being what all people are. I am pulled in the direction of romantic intimacy. That is really part of me.

But I am also drawn to a real celibate presence to people. It appeals to me. The part of me that is drawn to a celibate life finds expression in the song "Cherish." It speaks to me of being what all people are and yet accepting even the death that a celibate life requires.

I must have listened to the song a hundred times before I heard that the first verse is "cherish" and the second is "perish." "Cherish" is the word which describes the feelings within me, the feelings which make me want to hold another and mold another into one who would feel the same way about me. Then the song goes on to express my realization that "perish" is the word which more accurately represents the way my life really is. Even though the feelings for romantic intimacy are within me, those feelings must perish as I realize I am not going to be the one who will share the life of someone I cherish. And that is my choice.

So I am pulled in the direction of romantic intimacy. That is really part of who I am. But I am committed to a real celibate presence to people. I don't expect that the appeal of a celibate life will ever diminish my attraction to romantic intimacy. This is a tension I live with. And through accepting even death (I cannot seek out romantic intimacy), I can experience a newness of life (the real celibate presence I offer to people).

Living with these two realities inside of me is somehow captured in the song "Send In the Clowns." It's not the words of the song as much as it is the whole situation of being a clown that gives meaning to my being what all people are and my accepting even death. Actually, it's the whole clown motif which expresses how I feel as a celibate man in this circus called life.

Lots of my friends know I like "Send In the Clowns." Not all know just why I like it so much. Lester, one of our provincial councillors, gave me a tape with four versions of the song. And at one of our provincial council meetings, Al, another councillor, shared some of what he had learned about the meaning of clowning.

He said that the clown's original purpose was to keep the king from taking himself too seriously—the court jester. In modern-day clowning the clown is not a performer in the circus; rather, he or she identifies with the audience. As a non-threatening person, often a hobo, the clown acclaims and applauds and draws attention to the performers.

The first thing a clown puts on is the death mask, the make-up which completely covers his or her features. This is because the person who is clowning must die. Then comes the colored make-up and the colorful costume! These are signs of resurrection to a new kind of life. It isn't merely the person coming back to life; it is his or her passing over into a new and entirely different kind of life.

And in this new life the clown not only experiences new life within, but also gives new life to the crowds as they watch the performers.

I didn't know all that meaning was there, but "Send In the Clowns" has touched something in me which cautions me not to take myself and my celibate commitment—at least the difficulty and delicacy of my commitment—too seriously. It speaks to me of my position and mission on life's stage: to become what all people are; and to do so in a way that threatens no one, yet catches everyone's attention. I am not to hold their attention, only to direct it. In order to do that I must accept death—even choose death—to my own "idiosyncratic libidinal needs," as Eric Erickson calls them. In doing so, I come to a newness of life, both for myself and for those I identify with in a non-threatening way.

Only once did I have any experience of clowning. It was on a Palm Sunday at Saint Felix Friary. Paul was the celebrant, and he cast me in the role of the clown. That's how he had me listed on the liturgical program sheet everybody in the congregation had in his hands! And my role was to try to help the worshippers not to take themselves too seriously in their worship, to help them to enter the mystery by celebrating the liturgy less self-consciously than is normal for a group of Sunday worshippers.

I began my role by being me—Keith Clark. And everyone in that congregation knew me. I took that role and explained at the beginning of the liturgy that we would be celebrating the mystery of the paschal event by recalling the history which revealed it. I asked them to let go of me as they knew me and to allow me to be the spirit of history and to lead them in their celebration of the mystery. As I spoke to them before the liturgy began, I picked up the white alb which lay on the platform in the center of the congregation. As I donned the alb, I could feel them letting go of me. I could feel myself dying. I could feel myself taking up, for however short a time, a new life.

And I was free to do things with those people which I could never have done as Keith Clark. And they were free to allow me to do with them what they could not have allowed Keith Clark to do with them. My entire role was to catch their attention and to direct it to the mystery they were celebrating and to the main actors who were re-enacting the drama of Jesus' entry into Jerusalem and of his passion and death.

And as I recited the stories, I could move and act in a way that invited those people's participation in the celebration of the mystery—a way I could never have done as Keith Clark. As I narrated the stories of the entry into Jerusalem and the passion and death of Jesus, Paul and the others who were taking the different parts in the story made the gestures and spoke the words which the liturgy required. As I finished the narration of the passion, I began to take off the alb. As I told the assembly that they buried him in a tomb in which no one had yet been laid and rolled a stone in front of the entrance and departed, I laid the alb back on the platform. And I, Keith Clark, walked over and took my place beside Paul to continue the celebration of the Palm Sunday liturgy.

It was a great experience. And I learned something from it. Celibate people are clowns, if they will become what all people are, and if they will accept even death. In doing so they will experience a wholly new life, and they will give life to others. "Send in the clowns! There ought to be clowns! Don't bother; they're here!"

♣ *Part Three*

Opinions

♣ Chapter Ten

Society and Celibacy

I think it was my eighth-grade teacher who told us in English class that we were never to begin a letter or an essay with an apology. So this is not an apology; it's a "disclaimer": I know nothing about sociology, political science, economics or social psychology. However, it is the blessing of my private moments, and the curse of my friends with whom I share my private thoughts, that lack of knowledge has seldom stopped me from having an opinion on a subject!

It was the cowboy boots, actually, that started it all. I have something wrong with my back, and it is helped immensely if I wear a higher heel and one that slants. I was told a dozen years ago I could get specially made shoes or cowboy boots. At the time, neither was acceptable; specially made shoes cost too much, and cowboy boots! Really! No one wore cowboy boots where I came from. However, the pain in my back increased and cowboy boots became more acceptable to me. I bought a pair. And I've worn cowboy boots ever since.

Eventually I found a brand and style which seemed to work best for me, and for the past six years I've been buying the same boot, simply ordering by the number designated for that particular style.

Recently, when we were trying to decide if we were going to have an oil shortage or a gas shortage, I placed an order for a new pair of boots. When I went to the store to pick them up, I knew I had had enough. The boots cost about twice what they had cost four years earlier. And they were made with a different, presumably cheaper, lining. As I left the store, thoughts about our runaway economy went stomping through my head.

For years thoughts have been running through my head about our world situation: energy shortages, strikes, inflation, wage and price spiral, international relations, import-export balance of trade, corruption in government and industry, and so on. It seems to me that we're in a mess. I listen to news radio stations when I drive, and I listen to our government officials, labor leaders, economists, political commentators, and "man-on-the-street" interviews (pardon the sexist language, if you will, but they're still called that). I listen to women's rights advocates and activists and leaders of a variety of minority groups. And everybody has a solution for that part of the mess which most affects him or her. I've noticed that the solutions almost everyone offers provide some advantage to the group represented by that individual. The solution also calls for some other group to give up some real or supposed advantage which it currently enjoys.

In economics I think the United States is always concerned that the gross national product goes up and that the balance of trade is always in its favor. Labor leaders are always trying to get higher wages or increased benefits for workers. Industry leaders are always explaining how the increased cost of materials and labor has forced them to raise their prices. One political party is always pointing to the foibles of any plan proposed by the other party. Nuclear energy advocates are always telling us that if we are to meet our energy needs for the future we must build more atomic reactors. Environmentalists and ecologists are telling us that we can't dispose of the waste from the nuclear reactors now in operation. And then there was Three Mile Island! Our government tells us to conserve gasoline. Then the oil companies lower their prices so we'll use up the gasoline surplus that has accumulated because we did in fact conserve. And so it goes.

All this has led me to think that there is really no hope of turning things around by some grand economic, social or political plan, or by some more laws and controls.

I feel some sympathy and some understanding for the viewpoints of all those people on the radio who think they can explain what is happening and how to improve things. I realize that the oil companies, the phone companies, the utility companies, and even the people who made my new pair of cowboy boots, are faced with increased demands for higher wages and higher costs for materials and even for increased dividends by their stockholders.

Two events stand out in my mind as examples of what seems to me so foolish: the Three Mile Island accident (although now they're calling it an "incident" instead of an "accident") and the crash of the DC-10 airliner in Chicago.

The accident at Three Mile Island has cost the utility company a lot of money in lost revenues, cleanup and repairs, and advertising aimed at keeping consumers' confidence. The company wants to pass all that added cost along to the consumers in the form of higher rates. If it doesn't, the company will lose money, and the stockholders will sell off their stock and the company will go under. Then, they tell the consumers, where will we be?

American Airlines is being sued for millions of dollars because of the DC-10 which crashed in Chicago. Where will those millions come from? From people who fly the airlines. Meanwhile, McDonnell-Douglas, the company which makes the DC-10, has announced a new advertising campaign to improve the image of the plane. The advertising will cost McDonnell-Douglas a lot of money, and the airlines which buy DC-10s will have to pay more for them. And because the planes will now cost more, the airline companies will have to charge higher fares.

It's all a vicious circle. And most people simply throw up

their hands in despair. It seems to me that it's time for some understanding of the whole process, some sympathy for the complexity of it all, and some indignation expressed in something besides rhetoric. Someone has to decide to live with less!

But who's going to decide to live with less when all of us are bombarded by advertising suggesting we really need more? Lots of people are debating what is the best source of energy to meet our increased demands for it in the future. But is anybody debating whether or not there should be an increased demand for it?

Television offers a remarkable example of the way our society operates. It costs companies thousands of dollars a second to advertise on national TV. And companies will spend millions to bring me a good program just so they can advertise their products every 13 minutes. Because the advertising costs so much the companies must convince me that I need their product. And when they've convinced me that I need their product they then raise the price of the product to meet increased costs of labor and materials. But now I'm convinced I need their product so I'm willing to pay their price! The companies also pay people to research who watches what programs and to research what it will take to convince that particular audience that they need the product. And guess who pays for that research!

I wish that on the same night Walter Cronkite and Johnny Carson—researchers have determined that they are the two most believable personalities on TV—would come back on camera after a commercial and say, "Do you really believe all that bull?" But they can't. Their salaries come from all that bull! And so, on it goes, everyone looking for the villains who are ripping us all off, and everyone convinced that he or she is a victim, not a villain.

One morning over a bowl of Cheerios I was asking myself questions too weighty for me to answer. I do that at breakfast sometimes. Can a man, I asked myself, who has been seduced into altering the way he looks, smells and feels; a man who has been seduced into wearing a certain style of clothing and grooming a certain way; a man who has primped, plucked, powdered, sprayed, smeared, brushed, washed and gargled because he's been convinced he needs to do all this; a man who protests his absolute freedom to choose his toothpaste, soap, mouthwash, deodorant, shampoo, hair dye, clothing, and even his breakfast cereal; can such a man, I asked myself, ever decide to live with less? And can any woman do so more easily?

It is by having and doing all these things that people believe they are attractive to others who have also been seduced into believing that anyone who is anybody looks, smells, feel and sounds that way!

In my more pessimistic moments I wonder if we think anymore. And if we do think, whose thoughts do we think? We're not stupid or incompetent; that can't be the problem. But how we think and what we think seem to be determined by outside forces and influences.

Even what we think about ourselves as celibate religious people is influenced by those outside forces. The worth and meaning of our lives is often determined by the practical contribution we make to our world. Great causes which we espouse are often evaluated, even by those who espouse them, solely in terms of how effective they are in bringing about the desired change. And if very little change occurs, or if others do not get as enthused about taking up our causes, we get discouraged and perhaps even cynical about ourselves and the rest of the world. Then we go off and live arrogantly in our isolated, ideological ghetto, disgusted with the rest of the world.

I think celibate religious have a contribution to make to our society. I imagine diocesan priests have a similar contribution to make. That contribution is the *reflective living which a celibate life requires.* The vows and promises are a commitment to pursue the uncovering of the deepest possible meaning of things, persons and events. If we return continually to the solitary presence to God which our lifestyle demands, we will come to know that to have things is not the ultimate meaning of those things; attracting people to ourselves is not the purpose for which those people were created; and having events go in a way which is advantageous to ourselves is not necessarily an indication that they have gone the way they should have.

Celibacy is a lifestyle, not a ministry, that shapes our attitudes, actions, perceptions and to some degree, even our feelings about things, persons and events. It is a lifestyle of searching for their deepest possible meanings, a lifestyle of service to our church and our world. But celibacy is not service-oriented any more than marriage is. To think of celibate religious life only in terms of the ministry which flows from it, is to miss its meaning and to begin a long walk to frustration.

Some celibates who are led to recognize the deeper meaning of things, persons and events, take up ministry in service of others. As they begin to grow in appreciation of their ministry, they feel that pursuing celibate life in a religious community unnecessarily confines their passion for their ministry. Their frustration can be heightened because those who share their lifestyle do not take up the same ministry. And they may also meet some group outside their community who is as involved as they are in that ministry. The temptation can be strong to abandon the religious celibate lifestyle and link up with those in the same ministry. The many I know who have done this seem to me to neglect the fact that in living the celibate life their interest in ministry was spawned.

There is indeed a significant freedom and availability for ministry which flows from the celibate lifestyle. But it is not an absolute freedom or availability. Lifestyle must be pursued as lifestyle if any ministry is to endure. Neglect of the lifestyle in favor of ministry will see the destruction of both.

All celibate people are committed to a chaste and respectful love for the other human beings in their lives. Religious vow obedience and diocesan priests promise obedience to their bishops in dealing with the events of their lives. Religious vow to live poverty. Diocesan priests are urged to live simply by the directives of the church and the example of some bishops. A celibate commitment which is not embedded in a simplicity of life, a respect for others, and an attentive listening to the meaning of life's events loses much of its prophetic witness.

If we reflect deeply enough and regularly enough, we may actually begin to change the way we live. And our celibate witness to our world might become very clear, if we live with less in a relaxed and joyful way; if we meet and deal with people respectfully while being attentive to their needs instead of our own; if we accept and even advocate a turn of events which is not to our personal advantage.

Someone has got to decide to live with less! Someone has got to say "Bull!" to some of our society's assumptions. And why couldn't that someone be a celibate man or woman? We could be awfully good at it since our life is meant to be prophetic.

Chapter Eleven

A Word Eventually Has to Mean *Something*

For almost 10 years I have believed something I once read: that these times could be characterized by a "crisis of meaning." Ten years ago I took these words to mean that much of what we did in religious life, in the church, even in our society and culture had little meaning anyone could recall. People simply went through the motions without knowing why. Perhaps the crisis went even deeper; maybe the reasons which inspired certain activities were forgotten and no longer relevant. Perhaps people did things and there was indeed no meaning to them even though at one time there had been a very good reason for the activities.

I heard a story once about a new bride who on that fateful evening when she first had her in-laws over for dinner prepared a ham. Her husband watched all the preparations, including the rather meticulous way his wife cut off both ends of the ham before she put it in the roaster. "Why do you do that?" he asked. "That's the way mother does it," his wife answered.

The dinner was a great success, the ham an absolute delight. The father-in-law commented that it was the best he ever had. What was his new daughter-in-law's secret? The husband proudly told of the little trick of cutting off both ends of the ham before it was put in the roaster. That was the only difference he had noticed in its preparation and that of the many ham dinners he had eaten in his parents' home.

Since no one could understand why that little twist in the preparation should make all the difference, the newly-weds asked her mother why she cut the ends off the ham before she put it into the roaster. "Because that's the way your grandmother did it," came the answer. But the mystery remained.

On the first chance they had, the couple asked Grandmother why she had always cut the ends off the ham before she put it into the roaster. "Because my roaster was too small," Grandmother said!

We've lived through at least 10 or 15 years discovering that some of what we've done for generations, even for hundreds of years, has lost its meaning. The discovery caused us in some cases to search for the meaning once again. At other times the discovery caused us to stop doing those things.

Today I'm convinced more than ever there is a crisis of meaning. In some ways it's the same crisis which has been with us for a decade or more. But in other ways it has been compounded by the manner in which individuals have substituted their own meanings for lost traditional meanings. These new meanings have begun to alter the shape of the activities and traditions. There is not so much the void of forgotten meanings; rather, today's crisis is in some ways just the contrary. There are so many meanings today for the same reality that words can have just about any meaning a person wants to give them.

If today there is a crisis of meaning in the matter of a celibate commitment, it is not only the crisis of forgotten meanings, it is also a crisis of too many meanings. Celibacy is defined, described and lived in so many disparate ways that the word, the concept, the actual lived experience has come to mean almost anything from promiscuous arrangements devoid of commitment, to anti-social and anti-sexual attitudes and practices.

Some time ago I walked into Marty's room and asked him, "What do I say to one who has a celibate commitment and doesn't think that it excludes very romantic, even genital, relationships with others?" I don't remember his entire response, but finally he said, "Eventually words have to mean *something!*"

I have heard various notions of what a celibate commitment means. Some feel that a celibate commitment allows them activity short of intercourse with someone of the opposite sex, or "messing around" to the point of orgasm with someone of their own sex. Others think that all sexual responsiveness must be done away with and avoided at all costs in order to be faithful to the celibate commitment. They not only exclude seeking sexual response, but even the experience of being sexually responsive. The opinions range from understanding celibacy as merely a statement about one's marital status to a denial that one is in any way sexual. Some think it means they must deny their humanity; others think it means they don't have to accept even death. And most people, I imagine, are somewhere between these extremes.

I have had the opportunity to listen to religious men and women in formation and to seminarians preparing for the diocesan priesthood. They are aware of the entire spectrum of opinion and are tending more and more to simply pick for themselves some point along the spectrum, knowing that further experience may move them closer to one end or the other. There is something very tentative for many when they make their commitment to a celibate way of life. And the crisis of meaning becomes personal.

Seminarians about to be ordained deacons, I believe, especially choose celibacy for practical reasons. For one thing, it's a practical necessity to do so if they wish to be ordained. They also see its practical value for ministry. I have thought at times that our church is left with the disciplinary rule of celibacy for its ordained clergy, but has lost the discipline of life which could lead one to be inclined to make a celibate commitment.

The church has never, to my limited historical knowledge, upheld celibacy as a value in itself. It has always promoted and cherished "celibacy for the sake of the kingdom." And it was always assumed that those who "committed celibacy" were led to do so because they had an overwhelming experience of God, an experience of the cumulative effect the years of praying and immersing themselves in the scriptures and the theological tradition of the church. There was a certain holiness of life and closeness to God which was presumed of those who were to lead the believing community in its experience of God in worship. The everyday community life of the Christians was to reveal God's presence among them. Their worship was to help them know that God was beyond their lives as well as within them. And so those who were to lead the community in worship, at least in the Roman tradition, had to prepare for this task through a discipline of life which enabled them to have an experience of God which would lead them to "commit celibacy."

Religious preparing for final vows tend to "commit celibacy" a bit more naturally than diocesan seminarians, I believe. They see it at least vaguely as a constitutive part of religious life. They don't see it as a necessary prerequisite for ordination, even though some religious intend already at the time of their final profession to prepare for ordination in the future. Religious tend to see some prophetic meaning in their commitment to celibacy, I believe. But they are often hazy about the connection of celibacy to their pursuit of uncovering the deepest possible meaning of persons, things and events. They tend to accept celibacy as somehow an essential component of their lives which they will hopefully understand more fully as they live out their commitment. And that, in fact, generally happens.

I think celibacy has meaning on many different levels of

the lives of those who have made such a commitment and who live it out. And I think that those meanings do become more clear with the passage of time, but only if those people continually articulate the meaning of a celibate life for themselves. If there is not the continual but relaxed attempt to realize and articulate the meaning of celibacy on all levels of life, something about living a celibate life begins to die. The meanings are forgotten and "going through the motions" sets in. This may continue for a lifetime, and the individual who successfully "goes through the motions" is the poorer for it. It is possible that that person will begin to look more closely at what his or her life isn't, instead of what it is. The word eventually has to mean *something* for the individual as well as for the church.

If I were to sum up my reflections on celibacy, I believe I would say a celibate commitment could be described this way:

On the physical and emotional level, celibacy is the ability to know oneself as sexual and to experience some considerable comfort with that knowledge. It is the ability to regard oneself as sexual without experiencing the internal or external demand to do something about it—neither the need or demand to make it go away, nor the need or demand to act it out. It is the choice not to act out one's sexuality in a genital or romantic way.

On the level of relationships, celibacy is the ability to cherish and nurture other people's being and becoming without establishing bonds of mutual emotional dependence with them. It means not to be married, and not to be pursuing the path which naturally leads to marriage. It is the ability to establish warm and deep relationships with others by loving them and by being loved by them in a non-exclusive and non-possessive way. It is a way of loving which allows the celibate person to say, "They and I are better off for our having been together, but no worse off for our parting."

On the practical level, celibacy is a way of remaining

significantly more available to cherish and nurture others' being and becoming because of the choice not to take on the responsibilities of establishing and maintaining one's own family unit.

On the level of social impact, the prophetic level, it is a way of living which seriously challenges the hedonistic tendencies in all of us. It says that an auto is not something to believe in, that you don't necessarily deserve a break today, and that self-fulfillment is not the ultimate meaning of life.

On the personal, spiritual level, celibacy is a commitment to stand ready to enter fully and vulnerably into life's moments of loneliness because God can be found concrete in such moments. It is a commitment to face the reality of our separateness and incompleteness and to allow ourselves to experience, however momentarily, that our own being and becoming is blessed by God, and to discover the radical all-sufficiency of God.

But dissected into its various levels and parts, celibacy cannot be understood, because religious celibacy is a lifestyle which integrates all of these parts and levels in such a way that speaking only of one or the other aspect of this whole will severely distort the meaning of the experience. And yet each level and aspect of it needs to be verified if an individual is truly to live celibacy.

And finally, on the level of Christian faith, celibacy is this lifestyle taken up and lived in response to a call or invitation one has received from God to live as Jesus did. The call to a celibate life is a gift from God. Celibacy as a lifestyle has never been upheld as a value by the church. It is celibacy "for the sake of the kingdom" which has always been promoted. It has always presumed that the individual who takes up the celibate life has had an overwhelming experience of God.

I am not proposing an "official" definition of celibacy. After many years of reflecting on the meaning of my own celibate commitment, I have generalized to suggest that these various levels of the celibate life represent what our church has upheld and nurtured throughout its history. This is the description that makes sense to me; I want to claim for it no more than that.

♣ Chapter Twelve

Developmental Celibacy

A commitment to a celibate life, like all other commitments, evolves. It evolves first through random happenings of early life which dispose one to consider the possibility of a celibate life. Perhaps no random happening is so influential as the family into which we are born and raised. A family in which being what all people are, accepting even death, and knowing newness of life are part of a daily diet, disposes our emotions and faith to recognize the beauty of any Christian lifestyle. Our church worries *now* about a "shortage of vocations" to the priesthood and religious life. What will it be like in the future when fewer and fewer people will have been disposed to see the beauty of that life because they were never exposed to the beauty of the Christian lifestyle of marriage and family? In my opinion there is a "vocation crisis," and it is perhaps the married vocation which is most in crisis.

Besides our experience of our family, there are other random happenings in childhood and youth which may contribute to the evolution to a celibate vocation. Chance meetings with priests and religious, maybe even the special care and concern a priest or a religious shows for a young person, could begin the evolution. Even the general acquaintance of the family with priests and religious may play a part. If celibate people have been a part of the family life in which a child grows to adolescence, there is at least the possibility that in adolescence the child will consider the celibate vocation as an option.

The general family attitude toward things religious is another random happening which may begin the evolution of a celibate vocation. I know one younger religious man who was considered a roughneck, a don't-give-a-damn, would-be has-been during his school years. But after that perhaps necessary and normal phase of liberating himself from home and parental influence, much to everyone's surprise he joined a religious community. The religious heritage of his home had survived the test of his adolescence.

Besides the family influences in childhood and early adolescence, there are the deliberate choices we are first encouraged to make and then make ourselves out of youthful conviction. Those choices which help us act for the benefit of others instead of our own satisfaction and self-fulfillment contribute to the evolution to a celibate life. And choices to act in a generous way in matters of church life may be a further contribution to that evolution.

Whatever the random happenings and choices in early life which may bring us to the point of opting for the seminary or a religious order, at that point we take up the responsibility of ordering our choices into patterns which are compatible with the life we are moving toward.

When people are in the later years of a college seminary or a theology program, or in the novitiate for a religious order, they are ordering their choices into patterns which lead toward an eventual commitment to a way of life. There is, to be sure, something still tentative about life in the seminary, the novitiate, or during temporary vows. But there is also something definite about it. These programs are designed to lead somewhere, and that includes a life commitment to celibacy. Some things can be learned and accomplished on the way to these goals. They will be learned mainly by experience, some of which will likely be the experience of failure. They can also be learned from others and from reflection on experience.

One of the blessings of my life has been the opportunity

to listen a lot to young religious during their temporary vows and to seminarians. I've learned a lot from them and from reflecting on what they've taught me. My opinions about the development of a celibate vocation are based on their experience and on reflection on what they have shared. This is the advice I got.

Life in the seminary and novitiate and during temporary vows is a time for learning how to become what all people are. It is a time for becoming somewhat comfortable with adult bodies and sexuality, its already adult physical aspects and not-quite-yet-adult emotional aspects. There are things to discover and to become acquainted with. And that takes time.

Sometimes simply having a body can seem like a problem to the 20- to 30-year-old. It's hardly ever put that way. But the experience of a physical, sexual response because of an understandable stimulus, or sometimes just being "horny" with no apparent stimulus, seems like the curse of a young religious or seminarian.

"I'm always fantasizing that there's a man under my bed . . . and I'm disappointed there's not. What's wrong with me?"

"I want so much to go skinny-dipping with the rest of the guys, but I'm embarrassed. What if I get aroused?"

"I'm so ugly. My body is like an 'L.' I'm so skinny and my feet are so big."

There's a predictable preoccupation with the bodily aspects of being sexual. But most religious don't know that it's predictable.

Often a person's sexual orientation also becomes an issue. Some people want to know and show who they are rather than live with ambiguity. But there is a danger in a celibate declaring what he or she is. Celibates cannot get the kind of evidence about sexual preference that others get. Pursuing romantic intimacy or emotional involvement is contrary to the lifestyle. On the basis of insufficient evidence, for example, a man may label himself gay. Years later, after experience and reflection, he will realize he is not what he assumed he was.

In general, there's a temptation to fake it a bit concerning sexuality. A fake romance, a not-quite-real show of comfort with one's body or sexuality, a show of "experience" which covers the lack of knowledge—none is abnormal for the 20-year-old. I still think it would help immensely if we "older" religious and members of seminary faculties could, without making a big deal about it, give some indication in our demeanor and our discussion that we too have bodies.

Dealing with relationships is another preoccupation for young celibates. Sometimes a celibate is the object of a romantic initiative by another who wants to know if "this celibacy stuff is for real," or why "a normal, good-looking person like you would want to lock yourself in the convent." Most seminarians and young religious don't feel very locked away. But being aware that their life choice is taking them in a direction incompatible with romantic involvement, they feel a little awkward. They'd like to have their friends know they are normal, but they have chosen not to give the evidence of normality their friends will accept. The questions begin to take on some importance if the seminarian or religious finds the person taking the initiative sexually attractive.

Some think their normal desire to socialize and to experience intimacy with their peers is a sign that they aren't called to a celibate life. Being physically and romantically attracted to others and having intimacy and affectional needs and capacities is "just the way it is." If the assumption exists in the minds of young celibate people that such needs and capacities inevitably mean getting involved in romantic pursuits, they may either avoid all intimate relationships in order "to preserve my vocation" or abandon the idea of a celibate commitment because "I can now see that it's not for me." And they may never know they were suffering from "a severe case of normality" which is compatible with a celibate life.

But, like celibate people of any age—and like people of all ages in any lifestyle—the young celibate person is called to accept the kinds of death which bring life to that lifestyle. A young man in novitiate sitting naked on his bed writing reflections on how simply to be himself is inspiring. That's the scene which greeted me one night when I received a "Come in" when I knocked. That seemed to me to be an honest attempt at being what all people are and at accepting even death. It sent me off to my room to pray.

I think the struggle for a sense of independence from others' perceptions and expectations is part of being tentatively committed to a celibate life. To be close to others, influenced by them, learning from them and being taken seriously enough by them that they can also learn—these are issues for young celibate people. Dealing with these issues can at times bring confusion and struggle. But it is also an enlivening and invigorating experience. There will probably never be a time when there is an equally invigorating sense that our lives are really in our own hands and we can do something with them.

I learned a lot from Dennis. A year and a half ago I knew that if I ever did complete a manuscript on celibacy, there would be a chapter on developmental celibacy, and it would recap my conversations over the years with him. But at that time I thought I'd call the chapter "Friends Under the Glass."

The image comes from Dennis' reflections as he looked at the photographs under the glass on the top of his desk. When he moved to Detroit, he took along pictures of people who were important to him. He put those pictures under the glass which covered his desk. They represented his rootedness and his relatedness to where he had been in his life.

Over the years he was in Detroit, he worked many projects on that desk and piled many things on top of those pictures under the glass. Sometimes he removed those things to reveal again the faces of ones he loved, sometimes adverting to them, sometimes not even noticing them. But the pictures were there for the whole two years.

A year and a half ago Dennis was 23. He'd graduated from college and was teaching in an interracial school and working with youth who were in jail. He was more busy than he liked to be, but he was managing well, though not to his own satisfaction.

I had first met him when he was about 19 and living in Milwaukee. I got to know him better when he was 21 and a novice. The one long, serious talk I can recall with him when he was a novice concerned the rector of our minor seminary who had unexpectedly left the order and the priesthood to marry. In many ways that shattered Dennis' life. The rector was a hero, the epitome of what Dennis hoped to be but never expected he could become.

I remember that conversation because of my admiration for this young man and because of my fear for him. I feared he'd be disillusioned and decide to leave the order. But more deeply I feared he'd set out to devise some pat formula so he would never again be disillusioned, a formula that would not be adequate for remaining faithful to his commitment to celibacy.

I remember I tried to tell him that remaining committed to a celibate way of life demanded a continued openness to God who gave the gift, so that the gift could be received day-in and day-out. I remember trying to tell him that after we've done all we can do in order to remain open to continual reception of the gift, we do not remain faithful to our commitment because of the precautions we take and the devotedness we muster. We remain faithful because we know it is God's gift we are living.

But Dennis couldn't hear that, as I recall now. He wasn't going to allow what happened to the rector to happen to him. He knew the rector had made mistakes and had neglected things. Dennis would not. He *would* be faithful.

Dennis and I had a chance to talk when he was 23. On the night we talked he wasn't talking about celibacy. He was talking about pictures of friends under the glass on his desk.

"Those people are important to me; but they're history now," he said. "I don't feel particularly bad about that, but it sort of surprised me. Lots of things change. That's just the way it is. I wouldn't have chosen to change those things, those relationships. I don't like to say goodbye. I always figure I'll keep up the relationship until we meet again someday.

"I'm called to move forward," he said, "to growth, if you will; to change; to leave things behind. I'm not easily motivated to change. Whenever I face a change, I begin to doubt my resources for the new things and places and relationships ahead. I get afraid. I fear I'm growing old. I can't be 23 again. I'm afraid about the people under the glass. I'm not rooted to them anymore, except in a historical sense."

I don't remember all the conversation after that. I do recall that he spoke of a nun he worked with and came to like during the previous year. She was about to leave her order, Dennis thought. That didn't surprise him. He said he could see it coming in the way she lived, especially in the culturally conditioned choices she made. But he still liked her and admired her for all the good he had come to see in her. He expounded a bit on the way people live and the way their living influences their choices and commitments. But he did so with a calm, evaluative judgment about what he had learned, not with a condemnation and an urge to manipulate the choices other people make and the way they live. He stated that he knew a bit more clearly, though, how he did and did not want to live.

It was at that point in our conversation that my own mind brought me back to the late evening talk we had had when he was 21 and a novice dealing with the departure of a hero. The difference between then and now was striking. Two years earlier his ideological tenets overflowed into life with many imperatives for himself and for others. He could condemn more easily those who failed to live up to his ideals and was inclined to manipulate his own and others' lives with formulae for achieving what his ideals demanded. Now he simply looked at what he had learned from life and accepted it. He still had his ideals, but they were tempered and honed by experience. He still made judgments about the wisdom or foolishness of the choices of others. But he was less inclined to try to manipulate the process of other people's choices. And now he could say simply how *he* wanted to live.

It seemed to me there must have been a lifetime between 21 and 23 for Dennis. He seemed to learn so much from the pictures under the glass. He made celibate choices and celibacy became for him, I believe, a lifestyle. It was no longer only an ideology to which he was passionately devoted. It was an identity he was assuming. He was taking his place in the panorama of people under the glass in a way of life which was a successful variant of the lifestyles which were open to him. It was successful in that it was a recognizable lifestyle lived in conjunction with men and women who were his contemporaries and his predecessors. But it was a variant of that lifestyle in that it was his own.

"I know how I want to live," he said. He did not say "how others ought to live," or "how others should have lived," or "how I should live." Just "how I want to live."

Our fascination with romantic pursuits comes from the level of our needs and fears, while the appeal of a celibate lifestyle addresses the level of our true self, that person we are when we are removed from the crowd, from the occupations of life, from our needs and fears. Those who think needs and fears play off against the true self feel as if they are in the middle of a giant tug of war. If they invite each side to pull they are bound to be tripped up. They have one end of the rope around their ankles—their needs and fears. And they have the other end around their neck—their true self.

The fascination with romantic pursuits can validly be

played off against the fascination with the glamor of a celibate life. But the fascination with one cannot be compared with the appeal of the other. It takes some living to resolve it all successfully.

Although there is a certain independence from others in developmental celibacy, there is a necessary interdependence between the younger and older members of a religious or seminary community. I had a good talk with one of my brothers recently, who is in temporary vows. He's questioning a lot of things, especially his continued commitment to a celibate lifestyle.

Among the things which he identifies as reasons for his questioning are these: he's "horny," he is recognizing an increasing capacity and need for intimacy, and he's hurt often by the lack of sensitivity on the part of those he lives with. He also sees some Capuchins who don't make sense to him. He formulates his questions this way: "Am I happy in this life?" and "Am I *called* to this life?"

His wonderings make good sense to me. On one level he is wondering if he is equipped for this way of life. On another level he is saying his choice of this way of life is in question partly because of how those who share this life respond to him. I think those are good questions, even the right questions. Yet another question I think he could raise is: "Am I enabling people to respond to me in ways which will meet my needs for intimacy in non-romantic and non-genital ways?"

To gain the kinds of answers he seeks—and that I think he ought to seek—I think he has to look in a couple of different directions.

To find out if he is equipped for this life, he should look to older people with whom he shares his life and who make sense to him. He should honestly share his doubts with them and ask them for the benefit of their experience. He has been comparing himself unfavorably with them, and almost any such comparison must put him in an unfavorable light, since the others have a lot more life experience than he has. But he should ask them to reveal what they can remember of their own growing up in the order and to share their experience. Together they can arrive at an answer to the question about whether or not he is equipped for this life.

I think he and his brothers in the order should look at the way they treat one another. Is he in a community which respects its members and which encourages closeness and intimacy? Or does it neglect those simple human things upon which all intimacy is built—things like mutual transparency and respect? It seems at least theoretically possible that people can be called to this life and still not be happy in it because they lack the support they require. Much of the responsibility for this lies with the community.

However, as I have already written, the meeting of an individual's needs for intimacy is partly the responsibility of the individual. That individual must make the needs known in a way which encourages others to meet those needs. I think this is done primarily by expressing our gratitude when others have met our needs, and not demanding our needs be met only in the way we want.

A jar of marbles is a jar of marbles; and a jar of grapes is a jar of grapes. Even if the marbles are as purple as the grapes, there is little similarity between them. A marble in a jar is indeed touched by the marbles close to it, but a marble gives no indication on its surface that it has been touched. Grapes are different. They touch each other much more closely than marbles do because they can bend, be bruised and even bleed a bit. Grapes must accommodate to each other better than marbles do.

A celibate community is not meant to be a jar of marbles. It is more like a jar of grapes. A person who enters a celibate community cannot be a marble in a jar of grapes. He or she must show that he or she is touched and affected by the others in the community. In a celibate community the members must be willing to show, not only say, non-manipulatively that they have needs; and show and say that these needs have been met.

Any celibate community needs the mutual transparency and the respect upon which all intimacy is based. The silence about how an individual is affected by the experience of being a member of a celibate community leaves each person thinking and feeling that he or she is the only one who has any difficulties, struggles or doubts; that he or she is the only one who has any joys, successes or appreciation. And that can lead only to discouragement.

I learned one more thing about developmental celibacy from a group of my younger brothers who made their annual renewal of vows one cold December evening. It was made more poignant for me because earlier that day one of my solemnly professed brothers announced he was taking a leave of absence from the order.

The brothers renewing their vows had prepared an evening prayer liturgy around the theme of God's fidelity. Not too long previous to the renewal ceremony, Father Herman had died at 78. He was an important figure in our local community, and very important to the younger friars. He loved them and they him. During the ceremony the friars who were renewing their vows recalled Father Herman's statement near the end of his life that he prayed daily for the gift of fidelity. And at the point of the evening prayer when the actual renewal of vows was to take place, the assembled group of friars marched in procession to Father Herman's grave. There my younger brothers renewed their commitment to a celibate life of poverty, chastity and obedience. It was cold and windy, and the Capuchin habits we wore were under layers of winter coats and sweaters. Gloved hands shivered as they, one by one, held the page with the formula for renewal of vows. I was moved, not so much by the ceremony as by my brothers' recognition that fidelity is a gift from God.

The period of temporary vows or the years of seminary training provide a time for us to learn God's fidelity, not to learn about it, but to come to know it. Once we have experienced the ever-present love and care of God through life's troubles and our struggles, doubts and frailty, we can arrive at the moment of making a life commitment. Having learned God's faithfulness from experience, we can say yes to the commitment that has evolved, not out of any sense of counting on ourselves, but out of an assurance that we can rely on the faithful God.

Father Herman's prayer for fidelity at the end of his life was not, I suspect, a prayer born of fright, panic or doubt about God's power and will to hang on to him. That might have been the case earlier in his life before he knew God well. It was born out of a deep trust which arises from an intimate knowledge of a faithful God and a profound sense of human fickleness. When we have learned God's faithfulness, we pray for fidelity with greater passion but without panic.

The prayer for fidelity is a sign that we have begun to learn of God. I think that one of the signs of readiness that a person should look for if he or she is contemplating making a commitment to religious life or to the priesthood is the prayer for fidelity made in faith and not out of panic.

When the prayer becomes "Hang on to me, Lord, or I will certainly slip away from you," and it is accompanied by a peace and calm in the midst of struggle and doubt, we have come to know that God is faithful and we need no longer fear life's troubles or our own frailty. The growing awareness that all good comes from God and that all God's gifts are good is a sign that we are coming to know God's fidelity. Then, and only then, are we ready for a life commitment.

Chapter Thirteen

Celibate Skills

The making of a permanent celibate commitment through a free and deliberate choice does not mean that this commitment will not develop further. At the moment of our commitment to celibacy we also accept the responsibility of actively developing that lifestyle and keeping contrary commitments from developing.

To accomplish this we need certain skills, presumably acquired in the seminary or in religious formation. The only major differences I can see between life "in formation" and the perpetually professed brother or sister, or between seminary life and the day-to-day life of an ordained priest are these. First, no one is liable to be "designated" to be in charge of the continued personal formation of the individual. Secondly, with no more "hurdles" to cross on the way toward a goal, it may be less likely that the individual will be as self-monitoring as in the past. In fact, the goal that has been achieved is the beginning of a life commitment to celibacy. The continuing pursuit of a celibate life now becomes almost exclusively the responsibility of the individual priest or religious. And I think there are some skills which, if they are refined, can be very helpful.

I've listed seven skills which in combination seem to aid those who live "successfully" a full human life as celibates. I'm not sure I have much to say about each that I have not already shared in some way in these pages. I present them here briefly as something of a summary.

The first skill I think of as "being a clown." It is the ability *to experience being what all people are* and *to accept even death*, and to balance these movements of the paschal mystery in such a way that we experience the fullness of life which is available to the celibate man or woman.

Part of this first skill is to resist gracefully the temptation to buy into the notion that we "have it all together," simply because we have ministered to others in a way they appreciated. "Being a clown" means that celibates can identify with all others in their experience of frailty and need. If we were to try to live a celibate life with the attitude that such a life comes only to the superhuman, we would often feel that ministering to others is a herculean task. And if we should experience failure, we might accept it as evidence that we never should have tried to live a life which is beyond the scope of ordinary human beings. At the point of failure, or at the point of having to face that our needs and frailty are as great as anyone else's, the "superhuman" view of a celibate life provides a way out. For we cannot demand of ourselves what is not possible for any. If we accept a view that our celibate commitment entails the absence of intimacy, the affective side of our life will someday erupt with a violence that may drive us to romantic intimacy.

"Being a clown" means having the ability to be what all people are and to accept the kinds of death which the lifestyle entails. It is the deliberate and skillful way of living with our feelings, needs, urges and capacities without demanding, but still accepting, the kind of human support which is required, which is available, and which is compatible with celibate life.

The second skill I can identify is avoiding perfectionism. It is related to "being a clown." This is an especially necessary skill at the passage points of life, particularly a year or two after making a celibate commitment, and again with the beginning of middle life. (It might be important later, too, but I haven't gotten that far yet.)

There will almost certainly be a disillusionment somewhere within the first 36 months after making a celibate commitment, just as there is in marriage. There is the dawning realization in the early years of a celibate commitment that perhaps at the time of making the commitment we were not what we thought we were. And having now recognized the blotches and misspellings and the grammatical errors that dot the pages in life's notebook, there is the temptation to rip ourselves out of the notebook and start over.

With the beginning of the middle years there is the realization that we have been less than perfect. I've been told, and I believe it is true of my own case, that for celibate men the sexual drive becomes stronger in middle years. While this sexual phenomenon is occurring, regret and resentment conspire to attack a committed life and bring it down just at the point when it would predictably bear most fruit.

The middle years bring the realization that most of life is over. Regret is born of the realization that there is much we have not become. Resentment springs up when we realize the limitations of our life and how meager our accomplishments are when compared to the fantasies about what we could have become.

Perhaps more profoundly than at any other period of life, the middle-aged person recognizes that the shape of his or her life is determined by happenings and events, many of which were in no way planned or chosen. And many of the choices that were made now seem woefully uninformed in the light of further experience.

And so a celibate man in midlife (I don't know about women) seems to himself to be the unwitting victim of a conspiracy of his own heightened sexual responsiveness and curiosity, and of the regret and resentment which well up within him. It is often not recognized as regret and resentment, but experienced simply as an impatience with life, an increased irritability especially with those younger than himself, and a general feeling of having been trapped.

Defenses against this uncomfortable position are varied. Some try to immerse themselves in those aspects of life which brought satisfaction in the past. Some intellectualize their sense of failure and begin to blame it on others who in the past encouraged them to pursue their chosen path. Still others simply begin to withdraw from the activities, people and interests of former years. Some even decide on a fling—get a little of what has always looked inviting! And some seem to try one of these defenses after the other.

Neither immersion nor intellectualization, neither withdrawal nor a fling will lead to the re-establishment of the wholeness which seems to be missing to the mid-lifer. Only a lowering of one's desires about what life "should have been" and an increased recognition of what one has become can do away with the perfectionism of looking at what ought to have been.

A third skill for living a celibate commitment is learning to allow others to minister to us. This skill involves assessing realistically what we can expect from a celibate life in terms of having our needs met, and knowing how to go about allowing others inside and outside the celibate community to meet those needs.

If we expect that religious community life or the diocesan priesthood is going to provide fully for our needs of intimacy, or provide at all for our urge for romantic intimacy, we will be disappointed. Or if we take up the celibate life and try to live it with a self-sufficient image of ourselves, we will act as if we have no needs. Eventually we will experience our normal needs for intimacy, affection, affirmation, and won't know how to make those needs known because the self-sufficient image has been accepted by too many people.

It is a learnable skill to be able to say, "You're welcome; thank you for saying so," and mean it when our needs have been met by another's expression of appreciation; or to say "Thank you" when we have been complimented on some gracious act or accomplishment. It is a learnable skill to recognize and express appreciation for what we have observed in the lives and activities of others. These are ways of allowing others to minister to us and ways of enabling them to do so. They are the ways of acknowledging to ourselves and others that we too have needs for intimacy, affection and appreciation. In this way we don't demand that others meet our needs; we enable them to meet our needs.

I guess I hadn't been doing a very good job of exercising this skill. I was surprised to hear myself admit, after my days of solitude and after the visit of a friend, that "I didn't know how much I needed that." I had gone too long ministering to others without allowing them to minister to me.

Sometimes celibate people fail to see that some of their own needs are met in the ministry they have chosen. For example, many celibates choose helping roles but fail to recognize that a large part of their motivation may be their normal need to engage others personally and nurture them. But they tell themselves that they have to "get away" from these others in order to meet their own needs, and then will be driven by these same unacknowledged needs to overextend themselves in their work and say yes to every request for help. Eventually they will think of themselves as "victims," or they will begin to think they have earned the right to have others "take care" of them. They will demand that others meet their needs.

A fourth learnable skill is the ability to understand and articulate what our life is, rather than what our life isn't.

When we made our commitment to a celibate life, it must have made sense to us. We could understand and articulate its meaning. But I learned in writing a book that the ideas that were large enough to fill my whole mind at the time I was trying to find an articulation of them, lost their importance with the passage of time. Reflection on new experiences must give rise to new ideas or we will be left with an archaic articulation for the meaning of our present life.

If we fail to continually reflect on the meaning of our life and begin to focus on what that life isn't, there is little chance that we will remain happily committed to what we began.

Celibacy is a gift, a gift of something living. It needs to be cherished and nurtured as it grows and matures. When a person begins to find no joy or meaning in the gift, it isn't that the gift has been withdrawn. It has just been neglected, and perhaps no longer looks like a gift.

The fifth skill is the ability to live a shared life. I'm not sure how this applies to diocesan clergy. For religious it is fulfilled in their visibility and transparency and connectedness to their communities. Perhaps the recent interest in support groups among diocesan clergy is the way to develop this skill in their lives. But I am thinking primarily of religious.

I heard a provincial generalize once when a 58-year-old sister left her community planning to marry, "If one neglects to share her life with her community, what can you expect?" A shared life is not simply residence or presence in the local community. It must include a visibility in our activities and a transparency in our thoughts, feelings and faith. All intimacy is based on a mutual transparency of people without the obliteration of any of those persons. A certain skill at self-revelation is necessary for the kind of intimacy upon which religious community is based. And this self-revelation needs to be done with someone who can be completely trusted.

Yet friendship is not enough. It is possible for friends to live together in a community with others or just by themselves, and still not share those things which nourish their common commitment to a celibate religious life. For a shared celibate life it seems necessary to be visible to one another in certain activities, especially faith, prayer and a celibate way of dealing with others. It also seems necessary to be transparent with one another with the meaning each finds, and the difficulties encountered in that life.

Some religious are in situations which require that they live alone. In making and carrying out such plans, it seems to me to be important that they maintain a connectedness with their province or order, or perhaps with their diocese.

Recently one of my brothers asked me what I thought of the plans he was forming to be away from the province for three to five years pursuing an education. I told him that to seriously entertain the notion of being gone that long without planning to insure his continued connectedness with the province would be foolhardy. I did not caution him against his plans to be away for that length of time; I cautioned only against failing to include a carefully calculated method of pursuing his connectedness, and to whatever degree possible, his visibility and transparency with his brothers.

Friendship with members of our community is very helpful, but it is not enough. Friendship can remain whether or not people remain members of the same religious community. Even if we have many friends in our province or order, when a significant number of people begin to ask, "Who's she?" or "Who's he?" something is being lost.

Visibility, transparency and connectedness are the learnable skills for living a celibate shared life by which we are supported in our commitment. Everyone needs support in his or her commitment. But, as Lloyd said to me one day when he was our provincial, "Support is a funny thing; it seems to come to those who try to give it."

A sixth skill is praying. It is a learnable skill to bring ourselves to God as we know ourselves to be. To learn to enter fully and vulnerably into life's moments of loneliness to find God concrete is a necessary celibate skill. A commitment to celibacy which does not include a commitment to continually renewed solitary presence to God is a celibate wish. The solid nourishment of our spirit in solitude, even when we are inclined to settle for the junk food of casual diversion, makes a life commitment to celibacy possible.

And finally, I think a learnable skill is to enjoy the simple, harmless pleasures of life. This is not to be confused with the pursuit of self-fulfillment. It is a matter of learning to enjoy those things which are available to enjoy, rather than chasing those things which are not available. The pleasures should be simple, not extravagant sublimations of those things we think we have given up in embracing a celibate life.

A word of caution about these celibate skills: They can be developed without great angst and effort. They are learnable, but it is probably a mistake to work too hard at their development. Even in learning and using the skills of a celibate life we must avoid perfectionism.

♣ Chapter Fourteen

Falling in Love

This was our third attempt to see *Kramer vs. Kramer.* In the previous month, in two different cities, we had arrived at the ticket window to find it was sold out. This time we took no chances. We bought our tickets two hours before show time. Then we walked into the Phoenician Restaurant, reserved a table for two and went to the cocktail lounge. The waitress took our order, delivered the drinks and took the $10 bill back to the bar.

And he said, "Now you're supposed to ask what else is preoccupying me." I had asked earlier when we had begun our five-hour drive and he had told me about his family and his plans for the next two weeks. As the waitress returned with the $6.90 change, he said, "I think I've fallen in love." Three quarters and a dime and a nickel bounced off the table and onto the floor as our waitress tried to set down the change.

"Oh, I'm sorry!"

"That's all right."

"Enjoy your evening," we versicled-and-responded.

"Now that ought to get into your green-book," he said, hunching his shoulders and exploding a laugh. We clinked our glasses. "Here's to the third attempt to see *Kramer vs. Kramer*," I said.

"I first saw her when I moved to Philadelphia. She has an apartment a block away from mine. She is very attractive. We met and she's very nice. After the first semester I went over to her apartment. And then she came over to mine. She drove me to the airport to come home, and Keith, when she said goodbye, I've never been looked at quite like that. And I've never felt so much like a *man*." I think he emphasized the word only slightly so I'd be sure to understand.

"So what happens next?" he asked.

"What d'ya mean?"

And he said, "You know . . ."

And I did and I didn't. "I don't know what happens next. It happens to you. I don't know how you'll experience it. You're unique and individual; you'll experience it your way. I can't predict what will happen. It'll just happen. You don't have any control over that. You can control what you *do* because of what happens, but what happens is whatever happens to you when you're in love. You will now make choices which are going to intensify the emotional experience of being in love or you will make choices which are going to help you maintain and pursue the commitments you've already made. That decision is yours."

"Your table is ready." We carried our drinks to the table, ordered one filet medium-rare, one Phoenician combination plate, and two Greek salads.

"You also get the egg-lemon soup with the combination plate."

"Thank you."

"You'll like it." She departed and returned with the soup.

"It just feels so good, Keith," he said. "I've never felt like this before. And I feel so selfish. I don't want to share it with anyone. But I knew I wanted to tell you. You're the only one I wanted to tell. Oh, eat your soup!"

"I'm listening," I said, "and I know what you just told me; and I appreciate what you've just told me; I treasure it."

The egg-lemon soup was good. So were the salads. And so were my feelings. "That's neat, brother," I said; "I feel so good for you."

"Thanks, Clark."

"And I don't think it's selfish; it's just private. It is all so totally and intimately you."

I was happy for him, not because falling in love is an accomplishment, but just because it is another part of life. I think he did everything right. He recognized his feelings. He acknowledged them. And he was enjoying them. Though I felt too analytical about something so spontaneous and integrated, I told him why I thought he had handled things so well.

He had recognized feelings which were simply there. He had not tried to induce the experience of falling in love; it had just happened. He was enough in touch with his emotional and physical level to know immediately that the emotional circuits were carrying a new and heavy charge. If he hadn't recognized his feelings, they would have wreaked havoc with him and everything he tried to do.

He had acknowledged his feelings. If he hadn't they would have short-circuited and come out in inappropriate ways, and they wouldn't have made sense. He would have had so many feelings about his feelings that not much of anything would make sense.

And he had enjoyed his feelings. If he hadn't he would have either refused to be what all people are or been convinced that he was less than he should be as a celibate. If he had begun by feeling guilty, he would have believed he had little or no control over what he did with what was happening.

And he had done a fourth thing right. He had told someone about the experience, someone he was bound to by a commitment and with whom he could be honest. If he hadn't, he would have run the risk of living in a fantasy world where his imagination would nourish the romance. Talking about it had kept the emotional experience in perspective and perhaps begun to diffuse it of its power to dominate his life.

Also, he was transparent with a brother to whom he was

bound by a commitment, rather than with the person he is emotionally fascinated with.

This kind of transparent sharing is a normal way of establishing and maintaining a bond of intimacy. It's better that he should establish that bond with someone to whom he is already committed than with a person with whom he could form a bond of romantic intimacy. All intimacy depends on transparency to others. If he becomes transparent with the woman he is in love with, the intimacy could be so deep and so strong, at least on the emotional level, that previous commitments would seem to pale in comparison.

If he were to do this while the fascination is dominating his whole experience of being himself, he would be pursuing romantic intimacy, not because he fell in love with her, but because he chose to become transparent, which is a normal part of pursuing romantic intimacy.

Even as we sat there eating our dinner, I felt very judgmental; but those were my judgments. *Kramer vs. Kramer* was excellent. As we walked out of the theater I thought I could understand why he had said, "It's about people moving through a crisis; not just coming to a crisis, but moving through it."

Friends whom I respect have challenged the correctness of the judgments I make about such experiences. By their questioning and in our conversations I have had the opportunity to clarify my own thinking on the matter. Over the past decade, listening to celibate people deal with their own experience as they leave religious life or priesthood has caused me to formulate my judgments about how to deal with falling in love. It is conversations with friends which have helped me clarify for myself why I make the kinds of judgments I do. I would like to spell out my reasoning step by step.

First of all, falling in love, as I have most often heard it talked about, is an emotionally dominated experience of fascination with another person of the same or opposite sex.

To have fallen in love in this sense does not necessarily imply any kind of intimacy at all. Intimacy is the fusion of personalities without the obliteration of any personality. It is brought about by the mutual transparency of individuals to each other.

This emotional experience of falling in love can simply happen to anyone, or it can be sought in conscious and unconscious ways. Without even being aware of it, people can set themselves up for emotional fascination with others because they think they "need" that kind of relationship. And for some time this emotional fascination can seem to meet their needs for intimacy.

When I have the experience of falling in love, I can begin to establish bonds of intimacy by becoming transparent to another. Telling a person, "I have fallen in love with you," is becoming transparent to that person. It is a self-revelation which could begin the process of romantic intimacy.

However, I maintain that it is a mistake for a celibate, or for one who is committed to a husband or wife, to make this kind of revelation, because it is a normal step in allowing a romantic commitment to evolve. Although the action seems like the honest thing to do, although it seems as good and natural and normal as falling in love itself, there is a difference. The emotional experience of falling in love happens; telling the other that it has happened is a deliberately chosen act. We have control over what we do with what happens and we can and must make decisions about what we do with what happens. If we already have a commitment, part of what that implies is to keep contrary commitments from evolving.

At the moment that my whole personal experience is dominated by the emotional experience of having fallen in love, any revelation of that fact to the person who is the object of my fascination becomes yet another emotionally charged event. It is difficult, if not impossible, to put that revelation into any expression which does not include the indication that I am currently dominated by the experience on my emotional level.

It seems a little like the case of a husband who is momentarily dominated by the feeling that he would like a divorce and reveals it to his wife. Such a revelation has ramifications for the relationship which subsequent days, weeks and years may not be able to erase. The decision to reveal a feeling which is just there, is a deliberately chosen act of allowing contrary commitments to evolve. Later, when he is not dominated by the emotional experience, such a revelation could have meaning which would promote the kind of intimate relationship compatible with his commitment.

By being transparent with someone we are already commited to, we indicate that we are refusing to be dominated by our emotions and refusing to let an emotionally charged event like falling in love obliterate our previous commitments.

I don't mean to imply that telling a person that we have fallen in love with him or her will inevitably lead to romantic intimacy. But if the fascination is mutual and we both reveal we are being dominated by our emotional experience, we will likely experience a romantic intimacy that is very difficult not to pursue.

If people who have commitments that are contrary to romantic pursuits do not put on the brakes, they are liable to rely too heavily on "roadblocks" to keep them from careening down the road leading to romantic commitments.

The roadblock approach is typified by statements which begin, "At least I didn't . . ." or "At least we don't . . ." And as time goes on the phrases used to complete those sentences chart the normal course of romantic intimacy. ". . . spend a lot of time thinking about him." ". . . see her a lot." ". . . go out of my way to be with him." ". . . see her every night." ". . . let our relationship interfere with my job and other social life." ". . . get so wrapped up in the relationship that I can think of nothing else." ". . . get real physical with her."

". . . have any kind of genital contact with him." ". . . sleep with her." ". . . have intercourse with him."

I have heard each one of these expressions over the last 10 years as I have listened to people with celibate commitments try to deal with a romantic involvement by putting up roadblocks instead of putting on the brakes. They tend to plow through one roadblock after another, always feeling sure they won't go crashing through the next one. But as each successive one is crashed through, the phrase becomes, "We've decided not to do that anymore."

Eventually both parties may agree to break off the relationship, but there remains the haunting wondering about how the other is doing. Knowing how difficult it is, and feeling some responsibility for each other's pain, both want to look in on each other.

The roadblock approach is a mistake not just because it leads to the establishment of romantic and genital commitments, and a breaking of the celibate commitment. It is a mistake because it is a failure to pursue the celibate commitment begun when the individual said the public solemn yes to that commitment. Using the roadblock approach to pursuing romantic intimacy is like "having the best of both worlds." The celibate remains convinced he or she is committed to celibacy and yet pursues the road which leads to romantic intimacy and perhaps to genital commitments.

Two people who have fallen in love and who have pursued romantic intimacy quite some way probably can't get out of it all by themselves, with only their own efforts to end the romance. Each needs a friend, preferably a friend to whom one is already bound by commitment. And each needs to know that the other person has such a friend.

Intimacy is not inevitably romantic. Romantic intimacy does not inevitably lead to genital commitments. But I think there may be a right way to pursue a celibate commitment when we have fallen in love. And I feel pretty sure that there is a wrong way—a way which will be a distraction, perhaps a

prolonged distraction, from pursuit of what we have promised to pursue.

Will everyone with a celibate commitment have the
emotional experience of falling in love? Will every husband
and wife fall in love with someone other than their spouse? I
really don't know. My moral theology professor thought so,
and I'm glad he told me it would happen to me. But I don't
think it is an inevitable experience.

I have noticed at times a tendency of some celibate people to lay themselves open very deliberately to the possibility
of falling in love. I have experienced a great tendency to do
so, particularly in moments of loneliness. I suspect married
people open themselves at times to falling in love with people
other than their spouses. Occasionally when someone tells
me that he or she has fallen in love I want to ask if it's the real
thing or "let's pretend." Sometimes people in small ways,
maybe even in ways they don't recognize, set themselves up
for falling in love and then pretend it "just happened." The
emotional experience is very normal, but the choices which
must be made in order to continue to pursue a celibate commitment or a married commitment are made more difficult.

People have needs and fears and capacities they can
draw on as resources for pursuing what they want to pursue.
I have come to believe that much of what is thought of as
crises in celibate life and crises in married life are more often
problems in dealing realistically and constructively with life's
moments of intimacy and life's moments of loneliness. If we
deal with those moments only out of our level of needs and
fears, neither a commitment to marriage nor to celibacy will
make much sense. The more we recognize our capacity for
entering those moments of life fully and vulnerably, and the
more we recognize that we are free in our exercise of that
capacity, the more we can anticipate sound married and
celibate commitments, because people with those commitments will have found God concrete.

♣ Chapter Fifteen

Receiving the Gift

Before I conclude these reflections, there is one more thing I want to say. It seems to me to be the most important thing there is to say about the celibate life. For all my reflecting on my own and others' experience, and despite the fact that the most frequent entry in my green-book on the topic of celibacy is about the profound reality of celibate life, it can be said in only a few words. It's this: Celibacy is a gift.

I write this chapter almost as a reflection and a meditation on all that I have written so far. I've done the actual writing of 11 of these chapters during a week of vacation and a week of retreat. I knew what I most wanted to do with my vacation this year was to put together a manuscript from the stack of excerpts I had been collecting from my green-book. And so I spent last week in a cabin in Wisconsin all by myself, writing as much as I could each day. This week I've been alone in a cottage beside a small lake in Minnesota, making a retreat, but still writing some.

I've reflected and written a lot these two weeks. I've tantalized my own mind with the thoughts and I've tried to tantalize others' minds with the articulation of the thoughts. I've shouted aloud on several occasions my thanks to God for the coming together of the thoughts and for their finding words. I've rejoiced and given thanks as I saw the chapters completed one by one, and as I saw the stack of finished pages begin to equal in height the original set of notes collected over the past four and a half years. I've tried to be faithful about taking time away from writing—times of just being still, and times for praying. But my preoccupation these two weeks has been with the thoughts, reflections and the words.

Something much more personal and spiritual moves over me now. And I want to share that too. I'm grateful for the gift of it all—the life lived in celibate commitment, its evolution, its pains and joys which brought me to reflect often on what I had lived. I am grateful for the sharing others have done with me and which has expanded and clarified my own reflection, and for the chance to share my thoughts and faith with others.

But tonight it isn't any or all of these things combined, nor is it the support and encouragement I have received from those who wanted me to get busy and write. Tonight my thankfulness is to God for his fidelity in giving me through all the people and events of my life the gift of a celibate call and the gift of a response to that call.

I can recount the beginnings and the development of that call and of that response. I can recall the people who directed me along the path, those put there as directors and those who pointed the way for me when I didn't even look to them for direction. I recall my many brothers who shared with me their own struggles, difficulties and doubts, giving me the courage to face my own struggles, difficulties and doubts.

I recall my mother and dad and the way they loved all four of us boys. I recall Father McCollow and his care for me. And Sister Dorothy, who kept me after school one night because I had been cutting up in her fifth-grade class. She said, "I've taken a lot from you because I think you may have a vocation to the priesthood or religious life; but I want you to know that I'm not going to take any more." She was the first one to ever say something aloud about a call to a celibate life.

I recall Crispin. He helped me as a high-school student to accept my body and my sexuality. He was also the one who knew I was going to be a Capuchin before I did. I recall Emil, who must be the most loving celibate I know. During high school he never manipulated us with ridicule or enticements. He nurtured my budding call to Capuchin life.

And Marty and Paul and Jerry. They won't believe it when they read these pages. They've been my teachers as few others have and if I know I've given life because I've accepted even death, I know just as surely that I have received life from them as the fruit of their own celibate acceptance of even death.

And Gerald. He helped me know that my desire for a family of my own was a "severe case of normality" and told me that celibate people give life too. And Peter, who promised me that I'd fall in love, and who assured me that it didn't mean I was not called to a celibate life.

And Vince and Jody, Jim and Eloise, Don and Mary, Tom and Ann, Jack and Dorothy, and Jack and Sue. Some of them know in their hearts that they are the ones who formed me into a loving celibate man. Others will probably never know what they taught me.

And Jan. At a time when I could have wavered, she called me most strongly to fidelity to what I had begun, "I want to tell you, Keith Clark, and I want you to tell your brothers, that you don't have to worry about how you'll live a celibate life. There's no way you take that to yourself to live it on your own. That is a gift from God to be cherished and appreciated. A gift has been given to you by your God, and your God is faithful."

I recall again that shoe salesman who told Dad that there was a seminary near Fond du Lac. For years I thought of that man every time I thought or spoke about divine providence. "Next to God," I used to say, "the one most responsible for my being a Capuchin is a shoe salesman I never met and whose name I don't even know." And 22 years later, while I was in a shoe store trying to do a favor for a friend, I heard the owner say, "Oh yes, Don Clark! He had a son who went to the seminary, didn't he?"

"Yes," I said, "I'm that son. Are you the salesman?"

And I recall tonight all my brothers who have decided to leave the order, and who shared with me the struggle of that decision. I thought at the time that they wanted and expected me to dissuade them. But now I know they shared their struggle with me not so I could dissuade them, but so I would understand them. I think now I can understand. I know they helped me understand myself. And I'm grateful to them and to their wives and families for their continued friendship.

Tonight I thank my God for all these people and events which I can recognize and through which his call came to me in striking ways. And I thank him for all those people and events which I recognize as less striking but equally sustaining of the call he gives me and the response he works in me. And I thank him for those events and people whom I may never recognize as his instruments.

Tonight I know it's all been a gift—every bit of it. There's nothing more to say. "You have been given a gift by your God; and your God is faithful."

⚓ Epilogue

I've completed a second book. I'm pretty sure I'll be in trouble with some people because of what I've written, but not with those about whom I've written. They gave me their permission to write about them and even encouraged me to share their experience in the hope that they could help others. No, I suspect some will wonder if I really know what I've said about myself in sharing my observations, reflections and opinions. I may regret having done so someday, but for now I've done what I chose to do.

I may also be in trouble with some who read this book and who disagree with my observations, reflections and opinions. I have a proud streak which inclined me to call the sections of this book "Perceptions," "Analysis" and "Suggestions." But "Observations," "Reflections" and "Opinions" seem more subjective. I mean to claim for what I've written no more validity than that; this is the way I see it now. Some will undoubtedly see it the same way while others will see things differently. I am grateful to those who took the time and energy to make sure that I was saying what I wanted to say, and who still let me say it in my own way. I am fearful of trying to acknowledge them by name, because so many helped me prepare this manuscript that I would surely forget someone.

Commitments, like seeds, take a long time to germinate and to grow to maturity. I have written these words and shared these ideas in the hope that they will help those who are watching their own commitment to a celibate life grow

and mature. Perhaps the ideas will provide an accurate articulation of their own experience or their own experience is
so different that they will be prompted to do their own
reflecting and articulating.

Over the past decade the people who have shared with
me their own experience of pursuing a celibate commitment
are the ones who have given me the courage to examine my
own experience. For the gift of their sharing I am very
grateful. In many ways this is their book, and I feel more than
anything else like a broker of their experience.

Frankly, I'm afraid you might meet one or the other of
them someday, and with a smile on your lips and a gleam in
your eye be tempted to say something like, "Oh, you're the
Paul Keith wrote about," or "You're the Jan I read about."
And I am reminded of the tree I set out next to a bathhouse in
Indiana which was cut down carelessly. I ask your respect for
those who have shared their lives with you in these pages.
Treat them gently; they have given up some of their privacy
in the hope that someone else would benefit from their experience.

Today five brothers made their first profession of vows
in the Capuchin Order. It was a grand celebration. Don and
Mary were there. Their oldest son made his first vows. Paul
was there. Jack and Sue were there. Others who had wanted
to be there couldn't make the trip. But I thought of them
all—Jim and Eloise, Vince and Jody, Jan, Lloyd, Jerry. What
I witnessed in the ceremony of religious profession made
sense to me and brought joy to my heart because of what
these people have shared with me. They have formed me.
They have been my support in living a celibate life. From
them I learned how as a celibate man I am to deal with
life—with trees and books and other people's children. And
to them all I am very grateful.